*Cooperative Learning
in Middle-Level Schools*

The Authors

Jerry Rottier is Professor of Education at the University of Wisconsin-Eau Claire.

Beverly J. Ogan is a fifth grade teacher at Sherman Elementary School, Eau Claire, Wisconsin.

The Advisory Panel

Carlita Beridon, Language Arts Teacher, Northwestern Middle School, Zachary, Louisiana

Helen Blythe, Resource Room Teacher, Kenowa Hills Junior High School, Grand Rapids, Michigan

J. Merrell Hansen, Associate Professor, Department of Secondary Education, Brigham Young University, Provo, Utah

Janis J. Kapp, Reading Teacher, Manchester Township Middle School, Lakehurst, New Jersey

Harry M. Peterson, Jr., Facilitator for Gifted Education, Eisenhower Middle School, Topeka, Kansas

Cooperative Learning in Middle-Level Schools

Jerry Rottier and Beverly J. Ogan

nea **PROFESSIONAL LIBRARY**
National Education Association
Washington, D.C.

Copyright © 1991
National Education Association of the United States

Printing History
    First Printing: March 1991

Note

The opinions expressed in this publication should not be construed as representing the policy or position of the National Education Association. Materials published by the NEA Professional Library are intended to be discussion documents for educators who are concerned with specialized interests of the profession.

Library of Congress Cataloging-in-Publication Data

Rottier, Jerry
    Cooperative learning in middle-level schools / Jerry Rottier, Beverly J. Ogan
        p.   cm.—(Aspects of Learning series)
    Includes bibliographical references (p.)
    "Stock no. 3068–0–00"—P.
    ISBN 0–8106–3068–0
    1. Team learning approach in education. 2. Group work in education. 3. Interaction analysis in education 4. Middle schools—Curricula. I. Ogan, Beverly J. II. Title. III. Series.
    LB1032.R68   1991
    373.13 '95—dc20   90–28854
                                                                    CIP

CONTENTS

PREFACE 7

CHAPTER 1. INTRODUCTION TO
COOPERATIVE LEARNING 9

Four Ways of Structuring
Classroom Activities 9
Comparison of Individual
and Group Work 11
Components of a Cooperative
Learning Lesson 13
Research on Cooperative Learning 16
Cooperative Learning in Middle-
Level Schools 17

CHAPTER 2. IMPLEMENTATION OF
COOPERATIVE LEARNING 20

Setting the Stage 20
Selecting the Lesson 22
Grouping Students 25
Facilities 27
Resources 27
Individual Accountability 28
Group Accountability 28
Social Skills Accountability 30
Creating Group Cohesion 32
Assigning Roles 35
Social Skills to Be Taught 37
Monitoring, Intervening, and Processing ... 37

CHAPTER 3. TEACHING SOCIAL SKILLS 43
        Why Teach Social Skills? 43
        How Are Social Skills Taught? 43
        Modeling Social Skills 44
        Teaching Social Skills
           Through Activities 45

CHAPTER 4. SAMPLE COOPERATIVE
               LEARNING LESSON PLANS 49
        Body Systems 49
        Thingamajig 53

CHAPTER 5. STAFF DEVELOPMENT 56
        Introductory Workshop 56
        Extended Workshop 59

APPENDIXES 64

        A. Cooperative Lesson/Project
           Planning Form 64
        B. Additional Sample Lesson Plans 67
        C. Posters 109

SUGGESTED READING LIST 111

PREFACE

Middle-level students have important emotional, social, intellectual, and physical needs that set them apart from elementary or high school students. Middle-level educators are often looking for ways to meet these needs while addressing the academic requirements. The "middle school concept" places a premium on the development of the affective needs as well as the intellectual needs of early adolescents. Programs on student advisement, interdisciplinary teams, and expanded student activity are all efforts to focus on these needs. We believe cooperative learning complements the middle school philosophy because it is a teaching strategy that focuses on the total development of the early adolescent. As M. Gail Jones indicates, "The components of cooperative learning that make it effective are also those elements that make cooperative learning developmentally appropriate for young adolescents" ("Cooperative Learning: Developmentally Appropriate for Middle Level Students, *Middle School Journal*, September 1990).

Research on the benefits and effectiveness of cooperative learning is plentiful and will not be focused on in any detail here. We have drawn on the ideas of major authors and researchers in this area, tempered their ideas with our own experiences with cooperative learning, and focused these ideas to benefit teachers of early adolescents. The intent is too provide middle-level teachers with information necessary to successfully implement cooperative learning in their classrooms. We encourage those who use our materials and reach a level of comfort with this strategy to peruse the writings of other authors for additional thoughts on cooperative learning.

Please take this information and modify it to meet your teaching style and curricular requirements. View the ideas as a springboard to foster new techniques and activities. Use cooperative learning to enhance your classroom and to broaden the experiences you provide for those special middle-level students.

We want to thank Chuck Jirka of the University of Wisconsin-Eau Claire, Donna Franson-Hitchens of the Green Bay School District, and Sue Fulkerson of the Eau Claire School District for their help in editing the manuscript. Their expertise was much appreciated.

Of special importance to us are the teachers and administrators in our classes who designed, taught, and reflected on their cooperative learning lessons. Through our interaction with them, we advanced our knowledge of cooperative learning. We are most grateful that they allowed us to use their work in these pages.

Chapter 1

INTRODUCTION TO COOPERATIVE LEARNING

FOUR WAYS OF STRUCTURING CLASSROOM ACTIVITIES

There are four ways to structure classroom activities: individually, competitively, small groups, and cooperative learning groups. Each method should be used on a regular basis to give students a well-rounded school experience. Some academic content may be better suited to one method; other content can be presented using more than one method. The teacher must decide which is best for that class, at that time, for that subject.

Structuring an activity individually means that a student will complete a task independently of all other students in the class. One student's accomplishment will not affect that of other students, and will not be compared to the rest of the class. For example, students might be assigned to read a number of pages on their own to reach a goal in reading class. Each student may have a different goal, based on individual reading ability.

Classroom activities can also be structured competitively. Whenever this method is used, there will be "winners" and "losers." The winners are the students who receive the 100s, or the A's, or the passing grades. Students perceive the educational system as basically competitive. Most students learn quickly where they fall on the winner/loser spectrum. Some will work consistently hard, day after day, to ensure that they will be winners. Others will give up. They see themselves in the loser category and believe they will never be winners, so why try? The majority of students are in neither group. They do not try hard enough to be winners—they believe they will not make it. At the same time, they do not want to be losers, so they do just enough to stay out of that group.

Examples of competitive classroom activities are easy to find. The spelling bee and all norm-referenced grading are two. Even when a teacher tries not to structure competitiveness, such as grading a test and attempting to keep the results confidential, students will ultimately compare the results with one another to affirm their status.

Small group work allows students to complete a given task while working with others, usually in groups of their own choosing. This method provides students an opportunity to get out of their usual rows of seats and interact with peers about academics. Small group work is welcomed by the majority of students, but it can also cause embarrassment for the student whom no one likes, or who has poor academic and/or social skills. This method usually results in one of four outcomes: (1) students may successfully complete the lesson; (2) sometimes the group gets together and one student does all the work while the other members copy; (3) students sit near each other but all do their own work; (4) the group socializes the entire time, accomplishing very little, if any, of the academic task.

Cooperative learning is very different from small group work. Just allowing students to work together does not mean they will work cooperatively. Cooperative learning groups are highly structured. They require planning by the teacher to ensure that problems of small group work do not occur. In cooperative situations students are expected to learn academic material and to assist the other members of the group to work on learning the material as well. Students are linked with peers so that an individual succeeds only when all group members succeed. In other words, students are expected to practice basic social skills while working on the material.

One has only to look at the world of work to see how important it is for students to practice working cooperatively. The majority of adults who are fired from their first job lose it not because they lack job training or academic skills, but because they lack interpersonal skills—that is, getting along with others. Current advertisements for adult job opportunities stress the ability to work cooperatively with others.

Cooperative learning consists of seven basic components: face-to-face interaction; evaluation; individual accountability; group cohesion; social skill development; monitoring; and processing. All seven components must be present for a lesson to be truly considered cooperative learning. Otherwise, the structure would be considered the small group method. Each of these components will be explained in detail in this chapter.

COMPARISON OF INDIVIDUAL AND GROUP WORK

For middle-level students, there are positive and negative aspects of working individually and in a group. The benefits of working *individually* include:

- being able to work at their own pace
- doing their own work and feeling self-reliant
- experiencing the self-satisfaction of completing the task
- not being open to peer criticism, and not having to conform to peer pressure
- controlling their own time constraints
- working in an atmosphere that is quiet and controlled.

The benefits of working with a *group* include:

- having access to more than one opinion
- experiencing increased communication, understanding, and broader vision
- being exposed to a variety of information and opinions
- receiving group feedback and support

- taking less personal risk—it is easier to "fail" with a group than to fail alone
- learning appropriate social behaviors needed to work successfully with others
- sharing the responsibility for the task
- having more fun while socializing around academics.

At the same time both methods have negative aspects that must be addressed. The drawbacks for students working *individually* include:

- experiencing personal pressure and fear of failure
- having a limited viewpoint that may hinder their creativity
- being unable to check an answer with others
- feeling threatened when asked to explain an answer to the class
- not attempting the work at all
- finding it less threatening to sit back and not try.

The drawbacks for students working with a *group* include:

- being distracted by an increased noise level
- having slower abilities and not participating
- finding it easy to get off the subject
- lacking social skills and creating situations that lead to arguing about conflicting opinions, making negative comments to others, or simply not getting down to the task at hand
- being dominated by a student with higher abilities
- having higher abilities and being "dragged down" by others
- taking longer to complete the task.

It is important to note that a well-planned cooperative lesson will be structured in such a way that many of the problems inherent in working with others will be eliminated before the lesson begins.

Clearly, there are benefits and drawbacks to each method. Therefore, it appears reasonable that neither individual nor group work should be used exclusively. To be successful members of society, students need to learn how to work in many situations.

COMPONENTS OF A COOPERATIVE LEARNING LESSON

The authors feel that seven components must be present if a lesson or project is to be considered cooperative learning. Descriptions of each component follow.

Face-to-Face Interaction

It is imperative that students interact with one another during a cooperative learning lesson. They must therefore be seated in a way that allows this interaction to occur. This can occur only when students can see the faces of other students, either across a table or, if tables are not available, in a group setting with chair desks pushed together. Sometimes the floor is an appropriate work area.

Evaluation

Early in the development of a cooperative learning lesson, the procedures for its evaluation must be formulated. Each person is held accountable for attaining the academic objectives of the lesson. Thus, one portion of a student's overall grade for the lesson or project will be based on the individual's ability to master the objectives. A second component of the final grade is based on the group's performance as a unit. There are a variety of ways to determine this—for example, obtaining an average of group members' individual grades or giving a single grade to a project. In some cases, a grade is given for the social skills development associated with the lesson. The important point to keep in mind is that the criteria for each component of the final grade for the lesson or project must be determined and communicated to students prior to teaching the lesson.

Individual Accountability

Upon hearing about the idea of cooperative learning, some people believe that only group grades are given, implying that individual learning is subjugated to group learning. The fact is that both are fundamental to cooperative learning. In a cooperative learning lesson, it is important for the teacher to know the extent to which each individual has mastered the material. This means that some measure of evaluation must be selected that will provide the data that allows the teacher to determine individual progress.

Group Cohesion

Coaches in all team sports spend considerable time with their athletes stressing the importance of playing together. They emphasize the notion of team play over individual statistics. Few teams are truly successful if their members do not play together. Likewise, in a cooperative learning lesson it is imperative to develop a "glue" that will result in each team's members working cooperatively. The essence of such a lesson is that members "sink or swim together." Success in learning vocabulary words, designing an art project, or solving story problems in mathematics requires the team to function as one unit. In the evaluation of the lesson, special attention is paid to the extent to which members of each group worked cooperatively.

Social Skills Development

Many teachers use small group activities in their classrooms. Few teach the social skills necessary to help students become functional members of the group. It is assumed that students can interact in a small group in such a way that positive results are attained from the group work. When teachers are introduced to cooperative learning, this area is quite foreign to them. Simple social skills, such as staying in the group, speaking in quiet voices, or using more advanced skills like paraphrasing or cooperative problem solving, require specific attention on the part of the teacher. The beauty of teaching these skills to middle-level students is the potential carryover to all parts of their early adolescent lives. Learning to treat others with respect, to become problem solvers, and to develop leadership responsibilities are very important developmental tasks for these students.

Monitoring

To complete the processing component of cooperative learning, teachers must know what to look for during the group work portion of the lesson. They must be aware of how well students are functioning as a group and assess the extent to which the social skills attached to the lesson or project are being implemented. Monitoring is not an easy skill to master. It requires a planned record-keeping procedure along with the skills of observation.

Processing

One of the main tenets of cooperative learning is to provide feedback to students at the completion of each cooperative learning lesson or at strategic points if the lesson extends for more than one day. In group processing, the teacher may ask students to discuss for a few minutes how well each group was able to function that day. Thanks to monitoring, the teacher is able to provide feedback on particular social skills that were stressed that day, or on how well the groups worked together as teams. Middle-level students need this discussion to help them grow in the development of their social skills.

RESEARCH ON COOPERATIVE LEARNING

The research on cooperative learning is extensive. For middle-level students, the following generalizations are significant.

Cooperative learning tends to promote higher achievement. This is especially true for average and slower students. While cooperative learning has sometimes been criticized when used with bright students, it has been found that these students continue to receive high grades.

Cooperative learning promotes the greater use of reasoning strategies. When students are required to interact with one another, they improve their ability to become problem solvers. Students at the middle level who are just beginning to function at the abstract level will find their reasoning skills enhanced by participation in cooperative learning.

Cooperative learning promotes a positive relationship between students. This is especially valuable for middle-level students as they begin to interact with a wider range of students of both sexes.

Cooperative learning promotes more positive attitudes toward subject matter. Many middle-level students experience frustration as they interact independently with their subject matter. The ability to discuss the material with others can reduce this frustration and build a better relationship with the material being studied.

Cooperative learning promotes higher self-esteem. Developing positive relationships with other students and achieving a higher rate of success will help middle-level students improve their self-esteem.

For a more detailed description of the research on cooperative learning, please refer to the Suggested Reading List.

COOPERATIVE LEARNING IN MIDDLE-LEVEL SCHOOLS

There are a host of reasons why middle-level teachers should consider using cooperative learning activities with their students.

Cooperative learning activities add variety to teaching methods. Early adolescents have an attention span between 7 and 12 minutes. This requires the teacher to change teaching strategies several times during a class period. Using cooperative learning as a means of teaching a particular topic will give teachers one more arrow in their quiver of teaching methods.

Cooperative learning activities allow students to move around. Middle-level students need to change their body positions continuously. Their inability to sit for long periods of time is well documented. Many cooperative learning activities allow some student movement, which is a way to meet another of their needs.

Cooperative learning activities help students show consideration for others. Middle-level students can be very cruel to others. They need to be helped to show consideration for one another. Placing them in situations where they must depend on one another and where they are taught social skills may result in their developing respect for peers.

Cooperative learning activities involve students in decision making and problem solving. Middle-level students are poor decision makers, yet they are faced daily with decisions of tremendous importance. They must be taught how to make good decisions. Any activity that incorporates decision making and problem solving is extremely appropriate for these students.

Cooperative learning activities provide social interaction. Teachers report that if opportunities for social interaction are not provided for middle-level students, they will simply socialize at inappropriate times. Often this results in punishment for the students and causes stress for the teacher. Cooperative learning, with its built-in social interaction, offers the opportunity for students to socialize around academic work.

Cooperative learning activities give an opportunity to take a risk. Many middle-level students will not take risks for fear of failure. One of the worst things that can happen to them is to fail in front of their peers. Reducing the size of the group to two, three, or four may help students feel more comfortable about taking a risk when opportunities arise.

Cooperative learning activities are less threatening in a small group for praise or criticism. Middle-level students have an intense desire to be like their peers. For many, to be different is to be inferior. Therefore, receiving praise and/or criticism in a large group can be extremely debilitating. Offering praise or criticism may not seem as detrimental to students in a small group setting.

Cooperative learning activities allow movement from concrete to abstract thinking. Because students must interact with peers of all abilities, cooperative learning provides an opportunity to move their thinking to an abstract level. Group work demands decision making and problem solving, and if students can engage in these types of activities, they will grow intellectually.

Cooperative learning activities allow opportunity for peer acceptance. One of the greatest concerns of middle-level students is peer acceptance. Their self-concept is formed through the actions of others. If they feel accepted by others, they will feel more positive about themselves. Cooperative learning, with its built in dependence on one another, is a natural way for students to gain this acceptance.

Cooperative learning activities give a sense of belonging to a group. Everyone, including adults, has a need to belong. Many middle-level students see themselves as outsiders. They are very sensitive to the many changes they are experiencing as they develop physically. Most believe these changes are happening only to them. Membership in a group, even for short periods of time, can help students to overcome this feeling of isolation.

Cooperative learning activities provide an opportunity to be sensitive to others' abilities and talents. Placement in groups with students possessing a variety of talents and abilities is a natural way for students to come to respect the differences that exist in others.

Cooperative learning activities foster independence from the teacher. Teachers of middle-level students should be concerned about developing learners who can work independently. One way to do this is to create situations in which students must depend on each other rather than relying solely on the teacher.

Cooperative learning activities provide an opportunity for developing new friendships. Middle-level students are often afraid to strike up an acquaintance with peers unless they are assured they will not be rejected. Placement in groups gives them an opportunity to meet a variety of students; as a result, they may find it easier to form a friendship with another student.

Chapter 2

IMPLEMENTATION OF COOPERATIVE LEARNING

SETTING THE STAGE

When teachers prepare to use cooperative learning in the classroom, they need to consider some basic assumptions. The traditional, often competitive, classroom evokes a specific mindset for students and teachers. For example, in the traditional classroom we expect students to conform to the following norms:

> Do your own work. Don't pay attention to others.
>
> Pay attention to the teacher. If you have a question, go to the teacher.
>
> Eyes to the front. Be quiet.

In a cooperative learning situation, these concepts must be replaced with a totally different way of thinking. Students begin to depend on each other, instead of always depending on the teacher. They become responsible for their own behavior, instead of depending on the teacher to structure external controls for behavior. They learn to listen to other students and to interact with them. Each should contribute to the group effort and assume responsibility for the group product. Students learn that the work of the group and what helps other group members will benefit each individual, and vice versa.

Just as students learn to work differently in the classroom, so does the teacher change traditional roles and attitudes. Generally speaking, the teacher needs to be willing to give up being the center of attention during the entire lesson. Students must be viewed as capable of learning from each other and must be permitted a certain amount of learning noise. The process of learning and working together becomes as important as the final product. And the teacher needs to believe that students are capable of motivating one another.

The role of the teacher changes in other ways during a cooperative lesson. The planning becomes more involved and takes more time. During the cooperative learning lesson or project, the teacher suddenly becomes free to circulate throughout the room and interact with all students, instead of being "chained" to the chalkboard or lectern, interacting only with the small percentage of students who normally participate during a lesson. Now the teacher offers more ideas, feedback, encouragement, and suggestions to groups to enhance their learning, instead of simply giving answers. In addition, help is given students to manage conflict and practice small group social skills. The teacher checks the understanding of groups, helps them summarize their learning, encourages thinking, and provides resources when needed to keep the process moving.

To use cooperative learning, teachers must create a climate that will foster the cooperative attitude before teaching a specific lesson. For example, they can ask students to help each other briefly during traditional lessons. Teachers must model listening to *all* students, and valuing *all* talents, not just good reading or writing. They can begin to give problem situations back to students, asking them for possible solutions or suggestions, instead of automatically solving the problem for them. Modeling desired social skills, as well as appropriately praising the skills in the classroom, will show that these behaviors are desirable at all times.

One additional way to influence the climate is by making the room come alive with cooperative learning visuals. Posters and bulletin boards that focus on various aspects of cooperative learning will promote such a climate, and also help to teach cooperative skills. A series of ideas for posters is included in Appendix C.

SELECTING THE LESSON

Almost any lesson can be structured cooperatively—from a short part of one period, such as the practice portion of the lesson, to multiday lessons. Often it is helpful to structure the first cooperative lesson around a nongraded activity, such as completing a scavenger hunt to become familiar with a new textbook. When students are successful with their first experience in cooperative learning, most will look forward to future lessons.

A partial list of possible lessons and/or projects that can be taught using cooperative learning follows.

Reading/Language Arts

- Arrange events from a short paragraph into the proper sequence.
- Compose a class story on a theme.
- Dramatize a short story.
- Map a content area chapter.
- Practice vocabulary words.
- Write and perform a play.
- Use the writing process (conferencing, editing, etc.).
- Prepare questions on a chapter or a novel.
- Create a newspaper.
- Brainstorm background information about a topic.
- Learn two Latin prefixes and ten words using those prefixes.
- Review a novel (find theme, plot, setting, etc.).
- Develop creative writing.
- Create a myth on video.
- Practice spelling words.

Social Studies

- Identify five flags and how they serve as symbols in the history of a country.

- Explore the powers of the three branches of government.
- Compare religions.
- Research national profiles.
- Study colonial life or some other time period.
- Do computer simulation work
- Study regional landforms.
- Create a travel brochure.
- Plan a trip.
- Complete map work.
- Research work and presentations.

Technology Education
- Learn the correct procedures for using a power saw.
- Design and build a project as a group.
- Understand safety procedures.
- Do storyboard production.
- Explore careers.
- Build carbon dioxide cars or rockets.

Science
- Use knowledge of known powders to determine the makeup of a mystery powder.
- Design, build, and modify paper airplanes.
- Explore simple machines and their effects on everyday life.
- Understand lab safety.
- Practice completing and converting measurements.
- Create models.
- Design a habitat for 10 animals.
- Identify rocks and minerals.
- Practice first aid.
- Balance chemical equations.

- Explore electricity.
- Complete lab work.
- Research work and presentations.

Physical Education

- Learn the rules for scoring and playing various games.
- Design and perform a dance, swimming, or aerobic exercise routine.

Music

- Compose a piece of music.
- Practice a difficult part of a piece of music before whole-group rehearsal.
- Memorize words for a piece of music.

Family and Consumer Education

- Plan a theme for a party or community project.
- Learn to use the sewing machine.
- Complete a foreign foods unit.
- Practice refusal skills.
- Research related career opportunities.
- Understand nutrition and its effects on the body.

Mathematics

- Solve story problems.
- Learn simple constructions.
- Find areas and volumes of various geometric figures.
- Order from a menu—calculate total, tax, and tip.
- Make correct change.
- Understand Pascal's triangle or Fibonacci's sequence.
- Explore number patterns.
- Complete and convert measurements.

- Explore probability.
- Gather data and complete graph work.
- Research consumer education.

This list represents only a sampling of lessons and/or projects that can be taught using cooperative learning. With some creativity, most topics taught in middle-level schools could involve cooperative learning.

GROUPING STUDENTS

When teachers use cooperative learning, grouping students can determine the success or failure of an activity. Placing students in groups takes time and practice; sometimes the most well thought-out plan can backfire. There are many factors to consider when planning groups.

The first decision is, how large will the group be? Generally, the larger the group, the more socially skilled the students need to be to complete the task successfully. Larger groups usually require more time to get organized and to complete a given task.

To get all students involved in their first cooperative learning activity, groups of two and three are very desirable. Groups of four lend themselves to activities where students may work in smaller groups of two for part of the task, and then join together for another part of the task. Determine the group size, then, based on the social skills of the group, the type of activity planned, the type of students involved, and the materials needed for completing the activity.

Students should not remain in the same group for every cooperative learning activity they participate in during the year. Middle graders need to learn how to work with many different kinds of people, so groups should be changed often.

After deciding on the group size, the teacher must look at the type of composition each group will have. There are many points to consider here. Groups will be much stronger if they are of mixed abilities. A group of three could be made up high-, average-, and low-ability students. A group of four could have one high-, two average-, and one low-ability students. Keep in mind the tolerance of extremely high-achieving students toward extremely low-achieving students. Often both of these types of students will do better with partners of strong average ability.

Groups should have a mixture of boys and girls. Some younger, more immature middle graders become so upset when they have to work with members of the opposite sex that they cannot seem to accomplish the task. Therefore, begin by having these students work with same sex partners. Older students seem to be able to cope with this more easily, but, again, it will vary from group to group.

Cooperative learning provides an excellent opportunity for students to work with peers of different ethnic or cultural backgrounds, or educational and/or physical handicaps. Middle-level students will benefit from this type of interaction.

When making group assignments, keep in mind the students who tend to be leaders and followers. Students need to practice both roles. Some have special talents and resources that should be considered, depending on the project. For example, students with the best speaking abilities should be placed in each group if the project requires an oral presentation; those with artistic talents might be split up for a project requiring a visual creation.

Finally, be sure to consider the best groupings to ensure the most harmony. The two worst enemies should not be placed in the same group, nor will best friends always be a good combination.

When determining groups, a helpful source of information can be the students. Have them complete a simple survey to indicate whom they would be interested in working with. Effective survey ideas include:

- List three people you would like to work with cooperatively and one person you would not like to work with.
- List two people you think you could help with math, and two people you think could help you.
- List one person you have worked with before whom you would like to work with again, and three new people. (Require students to make at least one choice of the opposite sex.)

This additional information may assist in grouping and may also alleviate some problems teachers may be unaware of. Grouping is most difficult at the beginning of the school year when teachers' knowledge of students is limited. It becomes easier as the year progresses, and as students gain skills and maturity. Groupings that were not possible in October may work very well in February.

FACILITIES

In order to work cooperatively, students must be able to face each other while interacting. When desks are arranged in rows, this becomes a difficult task. During cooperative lessons, desks or tables need to be arranged to facilitate face-to-face interaction. Students become very proficient in moving desks in and out of groups when using cooperative learning.

RESOURCES

When special resources are needed for a cooperative lesson, the teacher should plan ahead to have these materials available for students. As with other types of lessons, the number of resources will vary, depending on the topic.

INDIVIDUAL ACCOUNTABILITY

As mentioned previously, it is imperative that teachers know how well each student has mastered the objectives. Teachers can determine this in numerous ways:

1. Objective paper and pencil quiz or test
2. Oral quiz
3. Asking students to demonstrate an objective
4. Having students construct or create an object
5. A short or extended written response to the objective
6. Oral report.

Some of these evaluative means are more easily scored than others. However, these procedures are the same as those used with other methods of teaching.

GROUP ACCOUNTABILITY

Perhaps the most difficult task for teachers is to evaluate students on how well they have worked together on a lesson or project. Generally teachers evaluate students solely on their individual performance. For one new to group accountability, there are several important points to keep in mind.

When six-week or nine-week grades are determined, they should reflect a variety of activities in the classroom. Seldom would it be appropriate for all activities to be done using cooperative learning. Students must be given the opportunity to perform individually as well as cooperatively. In this way, the bright student who may be used to working alone will continue to get the overall higher grade, even though one or more group grades may be less than an A.

The final grade for a cooperative learning project or lesson is a compilation of the student's individual performance and her/his performance as part of a cooperative group. In addition, it may sometimes be desirable to include social skills performance as a part of the final grade. How to weight each of these components in determining a final grade is a decision that must be made. Perhaps at the beginning of the year, the group grade component will receive less weight than the student's individual performance. This may change as the year progresses. However, it is important to make students aware that the group grade they receive will be only a portion of their final grade.

Before assigning a group grade on a cooperative learning project, it is important to discuss with students why all members will be receiving the same grade and how these grades will be determined. Students must be helped to recognize that everyone shares equal responsibilities in the project. They realize that when all members do their part, sharing a group grade becomes a fair assessment of the effort. Thus another means of group cohesion is established.

Group grades can be determined in a variety of ways. For middle-level students, here are five procedures that will work quite well.

1. The group grade is equal to the average of each person's individual grade.
2. The group grade is based on *all members'* individual grades reaching a certain level of performance. For example, if all members have an individual grade higher than 60 percent, the group grade is equal to a certain number of points toward the overall grade.
3. If the *average individual grade* reaches a specified level, the group grade is equal to a number of points toward the overall grade.
4. One grade is given for a project and each member's group grade is equal to the project grade.
5. After students have worked on a lesson, collect one paper at random and all members of the group receive the grade from that one paper.

Varying the grading method occasionally will help students continue to focus on their goal of true cooperative learning. If the teacher has been consistently collecting only one paper from each group to grade, it is helpful to intermittently collect and grade all the papers. If the papers from a group do not match, students need a reminder of the cooperative goals that have been established, and the social skills being practiced. Without frequent reviews, students will return to their individualistic methods of completing projects and assignments. Teachers need to experiment to determine the method with which they are most comfortable and which meets their needs.

An alternative to giving points for the cooperative efforts of group members is to offer some tangible reward. For example, if all team members score at a 90 percent level or higher on their test or quiz, give each member extra computer time, or candy, gum, five minutes for socializing; or dismiss team members first for lunch. In other words, there are a number of alternatives for rewarding students for their performance as part of a group effort. All one needs to do is learn what class members treasure and use this as a reward.

SOCIAL SKILLS ACCOUNTABILITY

The following form shows one method that might be used to combine the academic evaluation of a lesson with social skills acquisition. It should be given to students at the beginning of the project. This will make it clear to students that they will be evaluated on their practice of particular social skills that are being emphasized for this lesson. (This form was used in conjunction with the Body Systems lesson plan on pp. 50–53.)

BODY SYSTEMS GROUP PROJECT EVALUATION

GROUP MEMBERS _____

TOPIC _____

A.	Presentation (15)	_____
B.	Study sheet (10)	_____
C.	Key (5)	_____
D.	Visual aid (10)	_____
E.	Resource list (10)	_____
F.	All members have a part; all members had an equal part in the preparation. (10)	_____
G.	All members share responsibility in grade (10)	_____
H.	Cooperative skills	
	Stay with group (5)	_____
	Solve problems without arguing (5)	_____
	Talk in quiet voices (5)	_____
	Treat each other with respect (5)	_____
I.	Roles (10)	_____
	TOTAL (100)	_____
	GRADE:	_____

CREATING GROUP COHESION

Creating group cohesion is the step in cooperative learning that assures that the students in a group will work together instead of letting one person do all the work, or having one student sit back and fill the role of "wood tick." Expecting students to work together just because they are put in groups does not necessarily produce the desired result. In each lesson students must have a reason to work together, and it must be clear that working individually will not allow them to succeed. There are many ways of creating group cohesion; some of them overlap. The more different types of group cohesion that can be built into a single lesson, the better the chance that students will work together and cooperate on the given task. Descriptions of the most commonly accepted means of creating group cohesion follow.

Goal

In every cooperative learning lesson students must see that they can achieve their learning goals only if all other members of the group attain the goals as well.

> Example: Call randomly on one member from a group to explain the group's answer. All members must understand and agree to the answer because no one knows who will be expected to answer for the group. Or have students sign the completed worksheet to indicate they all understand and agree with the answer.

Reward

Each member of the group receives the same reward if, and only if, all members successfully complete the assignment.

> Example: All group members receive computer time if homework is completed by each member for one week.

Resource

Each member of the group has only a portion of the information, resources, or materials necessary for completing the task and all members' parts have to be combined for the group to achieve its goal.

> Example: Assign each group member different pieces of information about a planet and then require individuals to combine their expertise to create an accurate model of the planet. Or, for an art project give one group member the crayons, another the scissors, the third the glue, and the fourth the directions.

Task

Sometimes a division of labor can be created to help group members complete a task. In most cases the actions of one group member must be completed for the other members to complete their tasks.

> Example: One group member writes down the problem, another does the multiplying, the third does the adding, and the fourth checks the answers with the calculator. On the next problem the division of labor could switch.

Role

Each member is assigned a specific job to be completed or a role to be played during the group time. Each role has specific responsibilities that the group needs in order to successfully complete the task.

> Example: Each group has a leader, secretary, coach, and materials handler. (Specific roles are explained on pp. 35–37.

Identity

Each group creates an identity by having a particular name, flag, motto, etc.

> Example: Each group creates a banner to represent the group that will hang over its area during group times.

Outside Enemy

Occasionally groups can be placed in competition with other groups. This may include competing for rewards.

> Example: Each group competes with other groups for the highest average score on a quiz. The winning team goes first to lunch.

Environment

Students must stay together due to specific boundaries in their physical environment.

> Example: The group is assigned to the carpet area of the room and all group members must stay on the carpet.

Understanding group cohesiveness may be easier if equated to a football team. A team has a *goal*, which is to win the game. Winning is also the *reward*. Each member has a specific *role* to play, or position during the game. The *task* is divided into plays, which each member must complete for the play to be successful. Each team has an *identity*, or mascot. The *outside enemy* is the other team. The team is required to stay on the playing field, which is its *environment*. No one player can win the game alone. All the players must do their individual parts in order that the team may be successful.

ASSIGNING ROLES

One means of creating group cohesion is for the teacher to assign each member of a cooperative group a role to play. These roles are selected to be in concert with the instructional activity in which the students are engaged. It is good for middle graders to experience various roles and their responsibilities. Appendix C describes posters that depict these roles and responsibilities.

Some of the roles that might be used in cooperative learning lessons are listed and described in the following pages.

Leader

Regardless of the group size, whether two or five, it is recommended that one person assume the role of leader. The primary responsibility of the leader is to keep the group on task. This may be a difficult job for middle graders since they do not always like one of their peers calling them to task. In addition, not all students at this level possess the natural characteristics of a leader. This role will need some discussion and direction on the part of the teacher.

Recorder

In most cooperative learning group activities, one person should keep a record of the group's activities. The recorder keeps a record of any material the group needs for reporting purposes, making sure it is in proper form. When appropriate, this person gets all group members to sign the final product. It is important to define the requirements for each lesson so that the recorder is sure about what needs to be recorded.

Checker

The checker can help the recorder by making certain that each group member agrees on a particular response.

Reporter

In some cooperative learning activities, one person in each group will need to report the results of the group's work to the entire group or to the teacher. The reporter is assigned this duty.

Reader

If the lesson warrants it, one person can be assigned the responsibility for reading material to the group. This can be a reading of the directions, a paragraph to be analyzed, or the final copy of the material to be handed in.

Calculator

In lessons that require mathematical calculations, one person may be assigned the responsibility for making any necessary calculations for the group.

Materials Handler

The materials handler secures any resources that the group needs to complete the lesson or project, oversees the handling of the materials, and returns them upon completion of the lesson or project. Assigning only one person in the group the responsiblility for obtaining needed resources is one way to keep down traffic in the classroom.

Questioner

One student may have the task of coming to the teacher if the group has a problem, question, or concern. This role can also help decrease the amount of classroom traffic during the cooperative lesson.

Coach

If the teacher is having students practice the social skill of encouraging, one group member might be assigned the role of coach. That student would have the responsibility for making sure that no put-downs are used during the work time, and would practice making sincere, positive comments to team members. This is a difficult skill for middle-level students to master; they need to learn how to give appropriate praise, as well as to accept it.

Additional Roles

A host of additional roles might be assigned to students in a cooperative learning activity. For example, the teacher may want students to practice the skill of summarizing and may assign one group member the role of summarizer during a work session. Many of the social skills can be introduced in this fashion by having one member responsible for using the skill.

SOCIAL SKILLS TO BE TAUGHT

The following page contains a list of social skills generated by teachers of middle graders who have participated in cooperative learning courses and workshops we have conducted. The skills are divided into basic and advanced. The basic skills are fundamental to any group work; the advanced skills should be taught to students when they have mastered the basic skills.

MONITORING, INTERVENING, AND PROCESSING

During a cooperative learning lesson, the teacher's role is different from that of most teaching situations. Once students have been introduced to the task at hand and they know exactly what is expected of them, the teacher takes on a new role.

Monitoring

During group work it is essential that the teacher spend time monitoring each group's progress. This includes not only being available to answer questions when necessary, but also check-

Basic Social Skills

1. Everybody helping
2. Helping students do things for themselves
3. Listening
4. Sharing resources
5. Staying on task
6. Following directions
7. Staying in own area
8. Using quiet voices
9. Keeping parts to oneself
10. Responding to signal

Advanced Social Skills

11. Treating others with respect
12. Consulting group before teacher
13. Solving problems cooperatively
14. Explaining
15. Praising
16. Displaying leadership
17. Sharing and contributing
18. Giving directions ideas without being bossy
19. Encouraging
20. Checking others' understanding of work
21. Playing own role
22. Paraphrasing
23. Asking questions
24. Sharing feelings
25. Encouraging others to talk
26. Disagreeing in an agreeable way
27. Giving everyone equal time
28. Compromising
29. Summarizing
30. Correcting
31. Solving problems without arguing

ing to make sure that the learning taking place is valid. It means, too, that time is available to offer suggestions, pose new questions, and guide students to enable them to find their own answers.

During these interactions the teacher also has the opportunity to monitor students' progress in practicing new social skills that are being stressed during a lesson. A simple chart, listing group names or students' names, along with the skills being practiced, can be used. Checkmarks can be made whenever specific behaviors are observed. Since the behaviors have been clearly defined and demonstrated, students will know what the teacher is looking for. Students will see that the teacher values the social objectives of the lesson just as much as the academic objectives. The information gathered during these observations is helpful during the processing part of the lesson.

Intervening

Intervening is another important part of this observation time. When the teacher sees that faulty learning is taking place, it is time to intervene. Knowing when to interrupt a group regarding a discipline/social skill problem is a professional call; there are no hard-and-fast rules. The teacher must decide if a student is too disruptive to stay in a group, and when it is appropriate to make the group responsible for an individual's behavior. It is important to remember that group growth will be enhanced whenever a problem can be given back to the group and members can solve it successfully.

Following are two situations that occurred in one of the author's classes. The first example indicates how to let the group resolve the problem.

> Students were working on a project. The team leader came to the teacher complaining that Johnny wouldn't come out from under the table and the team was unable to complete the task without him. The teacher wanted to know why Johnny was under

> the table; the team leader was unable to explain. The teacher suggested that this information was needed to solve the problem. The team leader returned to the group, and within minutes Johnny was out from under the table and the team was working cooperatively.

In this situation the teacher knew Johnny and his need for attention. The teacher could have gone to the group and solved the problem easily; instead the team solved the problem by confronting Johnny by simply asking him why he had to be under the table.

In the second example, a team leader came to the teacher complaining that one student had not been completing the work she had been assigned, and the entire team was unable to continue to work due to this problem. This student had caused problems during group work before, and had been removed more than once.

> Annie was having many personal problems, and it seemed that responsibility to a group was beyond her ability to handle at this time. The teacher removed her from the group and made arrangements for her to complete the project on her own. During the next cooperative learning lesson, Annie was told to work alone from the start of the assignment. When the next opportunity for group work came along, she asked to be given a chance to work with the group, and was able to do so with only minor problems.

Obviously, the goal is to keep all students working with a group whenever possible. But it is not always possible, and the teacher must use professional judgment to make the decision, based on the individual situation. The majority of students want to work in groups, and this is often incentive enough to keep groups functioning satisfactorily.

Processing

Processing is another item that separates cooperative learning from small group work. At the end of each day's work, and certainly at the end of a major project, the teacher must take time to process with students how well they are mastering the social skills. If teachers are serious about having students concentrate on and learn appropriate cooperative behaviors, students need feedback on what they are doing well and on what they need to improve. Taking a few minutes to address these issues helps reinforce to students that social skills are important.

Processing can be done in many ways; it can be as involved or as simple as desired. Group processing can be carried out by having each team discuss how it is doing on a particular skill. Teams members can give themselves a letter grade, mark themselves on a continuum, or write comments about their progress. It is important that the group set a goal on what to work harder on during the next cooperative session. These evaluations can be collected and compared to the teacher's monitoring notes. Or the teacher can simply ask group members to briefly rate themselves by having the secretary hold up the number of fingers the group agreed upon—one for poor, two for average, and three for super. Each group could agree verbally on a goal for the next day before the end of class. Possible questions to ask include: What did our group do well while working together today? How did we do on the new skill we were learning? What did we learn today? What could our group do even better tomorrow?

Processing can also be done individually with students evaluating their own progress. Or individuals can evaluate the members of their group. The same processing questions mentioned above can be used with individuals.

Whole-class processing can also be used. During the last few minutes of class the teacher can comment on the monitoring notes that were gathered, mentioning how many times treating each other with respect was observed, or the types of conflict resolution that were seen. Suggestions can be gathered from the class on what was done well, and ideas for improvement can be shared.

The point is not to take excessive time processing, or to create more paperwork for the teacher. It is simply to provide feedback so that students know what they are doing well, and what they should do to improve.

The following is an example of a form that could be used for self-evaluation after a multiday cooperative learning project. (This form was used in conjunction with the Body Systems lesson plan on pp. 50–53.)

STUDENT SELF-EVALUATION

NAME _____

1. Would you like to work on a project with a small group again? Why or why not?

2. Explain how you did as a group member. Tell me how you did in each of the areas—say what you did well and what you need to work on in the future:

    A. Staying with your group
    B. Solving problems without arguing
    C. Talking in quiet voices
    D. Treating each other with respect

3. List each of the members in your group. Tell how they did working cooperatively. Say what they did well and what they need to work on in the future.

4. What did you really like about the project?

5. What didn' t you like about the project?

Chapter 3

TEACHING SOCIAL SKILLS

Perhaps the most significant difference between using cooperative learning and other teaching methods is the focus on teaching social skills. Teaching social skills is one of the seven basic components of cooperative learning.

WHY TEACH SOCIAL SKILLS?

One of the major differences between cooperative learning and any other method of teaching is the realization that social skills must be taught in conjunction with the curriculum. Unlike cooperative learning, other methods assume students possess or will develop intuitively whatever social skills are necessary to complement the method being used.

Aside from the fact that teaching students social skills will assist them in learning the objectives of the cooperative learning lessons, it it important to realize how valuable these skills are for early adolescents. Acquiring them is a major developmental task for students at the middle level. According to research, students will have greater cognitive gain using cooperative learning. If the academic gains were equal only to those of any other teaching method that might be used, however, the fact that these students may have made some gains in the development of their social skills would be most impressive.

HOW ARE SOCIAL SKILLS TAUGHT?

Social skills may be taught directly or indirectly. For example, having students stay in their seats and keeping their hands and feet to themselves must be taught indirectly in conjunction with another activity. It is possible to teach some skills—such as listening, encouraging, and paraphrasing—directly, however.

When teaching social skills, three points need to be considered:

1. Be sure students understand the skill and its importance. Teachers cannot assume that merely pointing out social skills to students will ensure an understanding of the skills. They must be specifically defined, discussed in some detail, and modeled for students. Many middle-level students are not aware that certain social skills are important in their lives, much less do they realize their importance in a learning situation. Spending time showing students why these skills are important will go a long way toward setting the stage for learning them.

2. Teach the skill with plenty of practice. After a social skill has been introduced and modeled for students, it is often advantageous to have students practice the skill before it is incorporated into a cooperative learning lesson. Having students turn to each other and say one or more words or phrases that exemplify the social skill of encouraging will make it easier when they are expected to perform the skill in a lesson.

3. Review the skill often. The final caution is to review various skills on a periodic basis. While skills may be learned at one time, some may not be used for a period of time, or students may simply become sloppy in their use. Consequently, a review will be helpful for all students.

MODELING SOCIAL SKILLS

We have labeled one of the methods that can be used to model social skills SEE 'EM—HEAR 'EM—DO 'EM. This is a modification of the T-Chart described in Johnson, Johnson, and Holubec (*Cooperation in the Classroom* [Edina, Minn.: Interaction Book Co., 1988]). In this method, students are asked to list how a particular social skill might sound and not sound, as well as indicate how it might look and not look. The following example will illustrate this method.

The social skill to be taught is encouraging.

SOUNDS LIKE	LOOKS LIKE
We can do it!	Thumbs up
Way to go!	Eye contact
Good idea!	High five
Good job!	Nodding
OK!	Pat on back
Keep it up!	Winking
You're on the right track!	
Awesome!	
Good answer!	

DOES NOT SOUND LIKE	DOES NOT LOOK LIKE
Stupid!	Rolling eyes
Dummy!	Frowning
Oh no!	Turning away
Boring!	Glaring
Just do it!	Bunny ears
I'll do it.	Thumbs down
Why!	Body language
Tsk.	Slouching

Some would suggest that discussing what a social skill such as encouraging would not sound or look like is inappropriate. Many middle graders need to be told, however, that certain gestures and/or comments do not exhibit the proper behavior expected of students. When a social skill is introduced, a brainstorming session can be held to list the descriptors. The teacher can then add any items not mentioned by the students.

TEACHING SOCIAL SKILLS THROUGH ACTIVITIES

A number of activities can be used to teach social skills. Some of these activities are presented in the following pages. For each activity, a list of the social skills taught within it is noted.

Activity 1. Telling a Story

Students form lines of six. The person in the front of the line is given a card containing a short story. That person is to look over the card, then tell the second person what it contains without looking at the card, until all students in the line have been told by the student ahead of them. The last person in the line jots down the important information on a card. This card is compared to the original card given to the the first person in the line. If the comparison is reasonable, each person in the line may be given a reward.

    Social Skills:
        Listening
        Paraphrasing
        Explaining

Activity 2. Drawing

Each person is given a card with a different drawing of a polygon. Students then select partners, sit back-to-back to each other and take turns giving the partner directions for drawing the picture. The partner drawing the polygon can ask the other partner questions. When the first partner has finished the drawing, the second partner repeats the task using his/her card. Then the partners compare their drawings to the original cards. Drawings that are "somewhat" similar to the originals may receive a reward. An alternative is not to allow questions.

    Social Skills:

Explaining	Following directions
Listening	Paraphrasing
Asking questions	Using quiet voices
Keeping parts to self	Listening
Giving directions without being bossy	

Activity 3. Mental Gymnastics

The teacher reads a list of simple mathematical computations. Students are expected to compute the correct answer without using any aids. For example, the teacher might read the following: $2 + 3 - 4 \times 5 + 15 - 10$ equals?

Language Arts teachers could use dictation sentences for a similar activity. Other content area teachers may also find ways to adapt this activity.

Social Skills:
Staying on task	Being quiet
Following directions	Listening

Activity 4. Jigsaw Puzzles
(This activity is an adaptation of an idea from Cohen [1986].)

Pick out some simple jigsaw puzzles. Give each group member a bag with one-quarter of the pieces (for a four-person group). Members have to complete the puzzle without a picture of the product in front of them. Talking is permitted. No one may take another's piece and place it for him or her. Hints and encouragement may be given, but all members must do their own part.

Alternatives include having a no-talking rule or putting the puzzles together upside down.

Social Skills:
Everybody helping	Contributing ideas
Cooperative problem solving	Eliminating put-downs
	Sharing resources
Correcting	Being sensitive to others' needs
Being quiet	
Keeping hands and feet to oneself	
Giving directions without being bossy	

Activity 5. Classifying Cards

(This activity is an adaptation of Guess My Rule, reported by Cohen [*Designing Groupwork* (New York: Teachers College Press, 1986)].)

Place a deck of playing cards in the center of the group. The teacher (or a student) selects a particular combination of cards and secretly writes it down (for example, face cards, spades only, or alternating colors). Each student in turn selects a card from the deck and shows the card to the teacher and the group. If the card fits the "rule" that the teacher has selected, the teacher says yes. The card is placed face up. If it does not fit, the card is placed in another pile face up. Each person takes a turn until the group has determined the combination of cards.

Social Skills:

Paraphrasing	Sharing ideas
Listening	Compromising
Correcting	Checking others' under-
Asking questions	standing
Being quiet	
Cooperative problem solving	
Contributing ideas	

Many activities that involve one or more social skills can be effectively used with middle-level students. *The New Games Book, More New Games,* and *Playfair* are but three examples of materials that might be consulted for additional activities (see Suggested Reading List).

Chapter 4

TWO SAMPLE COOPERATIVE LEARNING LESSON PLANS

This chapter presents two samples of cooperative learning lesson plans. The first plan, Body Systems, was developed by Beverly Ogan and taught to sixth grade students on several occasions. It focuses on an academic topic.

The second example, Thingamajig, is a lesson plan that we have used with teachers when presenting the concept of cooperative learning. While it is not built around a particular discipline within a middle school, it could be used with middle-level students to demonstrate the concept of cooperative learning as well as to teach thinking and problem-solving skills. It is for the former reason, to demonstrate cooperative learning, that we use it with teachers in our workshops.

BODY SYSTEMS

The science curriculum in grade six is structured in such a way that the unit on body systems begins with a review of the eight systems that are covered in fourth and fifth grades. This plan allows students to prepare presentations in order to review each system. It is designed to allow one day to introduce the project and teach the social skills expected for the lesson, three days of cooperative group work, two to three days of group presentations, and a final day for the quiz and self-evaluation.

Before the project starts students are asked to list three of the eight systems (skeleton, muscle, skin, circulatory, respiratory, eye, ear, nose) they would like to work on, and to brainstorm questions about each of the systems that they would like to have answered.

The requirements of the project include: answering the

questions from the class on the assigned body system, preparing a presentation using the answers to the questions, using at least one visual aid during the presentation, and providing the class with some type of worksheet that allows students to apply the knowledge they receive from the presentation. After the presentations are completed, each student completes a quiz based on the information from the presentations.

A. General Objective: To review the eight body systems
B. Making Decisions
   1. Group size
      Since this project comes early in the school year, it is felt that three students per group is a good size. It is not their first experience with cooperative learning, but they are not skilled enough to handle a larger group.
   2. Procedure for assignment to groups
      Teacher-assigned based on
      a. Ability: One high-, middle-, and low-ability student
      b. Interest in topic: Each student is assigned a system in which she or he expressed an interest.
      c. Sex: Homogeneous groups are used since some students have trouble working with the opposite sex. Mixed sex group work is saved for later in the year when students have mastered more social skills.
   3. Classroom arrangement: Students move desks into groups and put them back after each work session.
   4. Resources needed: Table for reference materials. Materials include books from the library on the eight systems, tagboard markers, filmstrips, filmstrip projectors, tape recorders, headphones, theme paper, note cards, transparencies, transparency markers, models, clay, and overhead projectors.
   5. Types of group cohesion: Role, task, goal, and identity
C. Preparing the Lesson/Project
   1. Academic

  a. Specific objectives
    (1) Use reference materials to answer questions on a body system
    (2) Organize information in logical manner
    (3) Give oral presentation to inform students and prepare them for quiz with a review worksheet
  b. Prerequisite knowledge and skills
    (1) Systems taught in grades 4 and 5
    (2) Review use of reference materials
2. Social
  a. Creating group cohesion
    (1) Task: Each student is expected to prepare and present part of the project
    (2) Goal: Group is able to complete an oral presentation on a system complete with visual aid and worksheet; all members must have a part in the presentation
    (3) Identity: Each group becomes known by the name of the system it is working on.
  b. Role assignment and responsibilities
  Teacher assigns roles for each student. Roles and responsibilities discussed before assignments made.
    (1) Leader: Keeps group on task, keeps all members involved in the project, is responsible for communicating with teacher about questions or concerns
    (2) Expeditor: In charge of all materials including moving desks and clean up; updates teacher on materials needed
    (3) Secretary: Keeps notes for the group together in one folder, completes task sheet as group completes steps in the project, records group answers on processing sheets
3. Procedures for creating individual accountability
  a. Each student must complete a worksheet from each presentation

  b. Each student must complete an evaluation sheet on each presentation
  c. Each student completes a quiz based on information from the presentations
 4. Specific social skills to be reviewed
  a. Importance of staying with assigned group during work times
  b. Importance of using quiet voices
  c. Meaning of the bell (signal to stop working, look at the teacher, and be ready to listen)
 5. Social skills that need to be taught
  a. Treat each other with respect—complete a SEE'EM—HEAR EM—DO'EM chart that defines how this skill looks, sounds, doesn't look, and doesn't sound
  b. Solve problems without arguing—teach steps in conflict resolution using a chart; keep chart posted throughout the project

D. Monitoring Procedures and Observation Forms
 1. Check sheet listing groups
 2. Keep tally marks when group members are observed treating each other with respect or using conflict resolution

E. Processing
 1. Group members evaluate themselves on staying with the group and on using quiet voices (first workday)
 2. Individuals evaluate themselves and group members on treating each other with respect (second work day)
 3. Class discusses use of conflict resolution (third workday)
 4. Students complete self-evaluation form to indicate their evaluation of themselves and team members on each social skill reviewed and taught during project (see p. 42)

F. Evaluation
 1. Individual performance
  a. Each student's part of preparation and presentation of oral report

       b. Seven completed worksheets and evaluation forms
       c. Quiz on eight body systems
  2. Group performance: Oral presentation
  3. Social skills performance
       a. Check sheet on skills
       b. Group processing sheets
  4. Procedure for determining composite grade for project
       a. Each group receives a project grade—a combination grade based on oral presentation and social skills used
       b. Each individual receives quiz grade: the two grades are not averaged

THINGAMAJIG

A. General Objectives
  1. To model the concept of cooperative learning
  2. To teach social skills such as cooperative problem solving, encouraging, giving directions without being bossy, explaining, everyone participating, etc.
  3. To practice roles
  4. To use all materials to create a unique object
B. Making Decisions
  1. Group Size: Groups of three or four work well
  2. Procedure for assignment to groups: Teacher-assigned based on nature of class one might be working with
  3. Classroom arrangement: Tables for each group are best or flat surface made up of desk tops. One additional table necessary for supplies
  4. Resources needed: One plastic baggie, three different pieces of cardboard (recommend one two by two-inch, one four by four-inch, and one eight by eight-inch), two pipe cleaners, four bobby pins, one rubber band, three marshmallows, four paper clips, one crayon, and one marker for coloring
  5. Types of group cohesion
     Role, goal, reward, resource, outside enemy

C. Preparing the Lesson/Project
   1. Academic
      a. Specific objectives
         (1) Participate in cooperative learning lesson
         (2) Learning skills of thinking and problem solving
      b. Prerequisite knowledge and skills: None
   2. Social
      a. Creating group cohesion
         (1) Goal: Each group must work together to develop a Thingamagig
         (2) Role: Each group member has a specific role to play
         (3) Reward: Each group member with the best Thingamajig receives an award
         (4) Resource: Only one group member has supplies necessary to complete the project
         (5) Outside enemy: Each group is competing against the others to make the best Thingamajig
      b. Role assignment and responsibilities
         (1) Leader: Keeps group on task and makes sure everyone participates
         (2) Coach: Praises others in the group and gives them support
         (3) Materials Handler: Collects the materials from the front table and handles them (the only person in the group who can touch the materials)
         (4) Checker: Makes sure everyone in the group agrees with procedures
   3. Procedures for creating individual accountability: Each person must actively participate in activity
   4. Specific social skills to be reviewed
      a. Importance of staying with assigned group during work times
      b. Importance of using quiet voices
      c. Others could be included, depending on the group

5. Social skills that need to be taught
   a. Compromise—Discuss the use of compromise
   b. Everyone participates
D. Monitoring Procedures and Observation Forms
   1. Check sheet listing groups
   2. Keep tally marks when all group members participate or use compromising
E. Processing: Class Discussion on Use of Compromising
F. Evaluation
   1. Individual performance: Each student's participation in activity
   2. Group performance: Development of Thingamajig
   3. Social skills performance
      a. Check sheet on skills
      b. Group processing sheets
   4. Procedure for determining composite grade for project: Each group receives grade based on individual performance as part of the group as well as performance of total group

Chapter 5

STAFF DEVELOPMENT

Many great educational ideas have been attempted; some have been colossal failures. One reason for failure is the lack of staff preparation. Cooperative learning has significant potential for use in middle-level classrooms, but it too will fail without appropriate staff development.

The authors are very concerned about the quality of staff development to successfully implement cooperative learning lessons. In our opinion, it takes a minimum of 24 hours of instruction to effectively learn all the components of cooperative learning. Furthermore, the instruction must be "chunked," that is, taught as an entirety before participants are asked to teach cooperative learning lessons to students. Staff development is strengthened if, after the initial instruction, participants are required to plan and teach a lesson and then return for a critiquing session.

This chapter presents two workshop formats that we have used. The first, a two-hour workshop, is an introduction to cooperative learning. No participants should be expected to teach a cooperative learning lesson upon completion of this session. Its purpose is to provide information to help clarify the concept of cooperative learning.

The second requires 30 hours of instruction. We feel that after this amount of instruction, participants should feel comfortable designing a cooperative learning lesson and, more importantly, should achieve a reasonable degree of success.

INTRODUCTORY WORKSHOP

I. Introduction of Presenters

It is important to establish the credibility of the presenters. Teachers are very concerned that the presenter(s) can speak from some experience utilizing cooperative learning.

II. Individual Versus Groupwork

We begin our introduction to cooperative learning by involving participants in three different activities. Groups are formed in advance to ensure heterogeneity.

Activity 1

Each member of each group is given a simple problem to solve. Problems such as asking participants to find the net cost of an item, given the original cost and a discount rate, may be used. Participants are told they must work alone on the project, without consulting their group members.

Activity 2

Each group is given a second problem to solve. Members are to select a leader, recorder, and reporter for their group. They are asked to solve the problem collectively.

Activity 3

Each group is asked to brainstorm the positive and negative aspects of working alone and of working as a group. If the total group is very large (we have done this with 200 at one time), each group is given a prepared list of positive and negative aspects of individual and group work and is asked to compare its responses to our list. If the group is 50 or less, we may have reporters from each group give us items from their lists as we write them on an overhead.

The purpose of these three activities is to acquaint the participants with the differences between individual and group work. Generally we find that the negative aspects of group work all relate to social skills. We point this out and recall it at a later time when we introduce the components of cooperative learning.

III. Introduction to Cooperative Learning

This portion of the workshop is a presentation covering the following topics:
A. Four Means of Structuring Learning
B. Components of Cooperative Learning
C. Research on Cooperative Learning
D. Implementing Cooperative Learning

IV. Reviewing the Components of Cooperative Learning

After the presentation, we involve participants in another group activity. The "Tribes Activity" was developed from a story found in *Learning Together and Alone: Cooperative, Competitive, and Individualistic Learning,* by David W. Johnson and Roger T. Johnson (see Suggested Reading List). Group members must read and study one part of the three stories and then teach one another. At the conclusion of the activity, they are given an individual quiz on the story. If all members of the group receive a certain percentage correct, the group is given a reward.

After the activity is completed, the components of cooperative learning are reviewed to show participants how all components were included in the activity.

V. Workshop Wrap-up

Two topics are covered in the workshop wrap-up.
A. A number of benefits for utilizing cooperative learning with middle-level students are presented.

B. At the beginning of the workshop and again at the end, we stress that what participants may have learned in two hours is not enough to begin using cooperative learning in their classrooms. A number of topics that must be studied in much more detail before implementing cooperative learning are pointed out. These topics are as follows:

1. Setting up the groups
2. Teaching social skills
3. Creating group cohesion
4. Monitoring
5. Processing
6. Evaluating

EXTENDED WORKSHOP

To learn the details of designing a cooperative learning lesson and gain the self-confidence that accompanies this knowledge, we have found that it takes about 30 hours of instruction. The material that follows presents the activities that have proven to be successful for us.

Each session represents a block of three hours. Modifications can be made, depending on the nature and size of the group of participants.

Session 1

The first portion of this session is designed to allow students the opportunity to get to know each other. Later in the class, we will ask them to work together, so it is important that they become acquainted.

The second portion is an introduction to cooperative learning. Time is spent explaining the four ways of structuring classroom activities (individualistic, competitive, small group, and cooperative learning). Participants are asked to brainstorm the advantages and disadvantages of working independently and in small groups. At the conclusion of this activity, they are introduced to the seven components of cooperative learning.

Session 2

This session begins by pointing out the research on cooperative learning. The reasons why cooperative learning is such a worthwhile strategy for use with middle-level students is the next item covered. Then some time is spent responding to often-asked questions and concerns expressed by teachers, administrators, and parents about cooperative learning.

At this point we initiate a step-by-step procedure for designing cooperative learning lessons using the lesson plan format found in Appendix A. We begin by pointing out a variety of lessons that can be taught cooperatively. Participants are then placed in groups according to various teaching disciplines and are asked to brainstorm possible one-day lessons and three-to-five-day lessons or projects that might be taught using cooperative learning. They share these lesson ideas by placing them on newsprint and taping them to the walls of the classroom for all to see.

Session 3

We begin by having the groups that brainstormed cooperative learning lessons in Session 2 select one of the three-day lessons or projects and write general and specific objectives for it. Sometimes it is helpful to review how to write general and specific objectives.

Next we cover decisions about group size and assignment. Each group size is discussed, paying particular attention to the nature of middle-level students. This is followed by consideration of a variety of ways of assigning students to groups. Then, participants are given a hypothetical class and told to select the group size and to decide to place students into the groups. Participants usually find this rather difficult to do. We follow up this activity with a discussion of their decisions.

Session 4

Arranging the cooperative learning classroom and determining resources necessary for conducting cooperative learning are the first items on the agenda for this session. This is followed by an introduction to creating group cohesion, which is taught using cooperative groups. We place participants in groups and have them teach each other a number of ways of creating group cohesion. At the conclusion, each person must take a quiz and each group is given some type of reward if each group member gets 90 or better on the quiz. Generally this creates an excellent discussion of the topic.

Assignment of roles in cooperative learning groups is the last topic covered in this session.

Before concluding this session, we ask participants to spend five minutes writing their reactions to the first four sessions. They are encouraged to list any questions or concerns they may have at this point. Their material is collected and analyzed by the instructors prior to the next session.

In addition, participants are given copies of several articles to read for the next session. These articles are given in the Suggested Reading List.

Session 5

This session begins with responses to any questions or concerns that participants have raised. Afterward, participants are placed in small groups, asked to discuss one of the articles assigned at the end of the previous session, and then to share the major points of the articles.

To help participants develop a detailed cooperative learning lesson plan, a portion of a lesson plan on Body Systems (see pp. 50–53) is done for them on the overhead. They are asked to work in their groups from Session 3 and complete the lesson plan form parts A through C. 2.

Session 6

The class begins by having all groups give a short report on the progress of the lesson plans they are working on.

The next item covered is the concept of structuring individual accountability. This does not seem to cause too much difficulty since it is similar to procedures participants use in their classrooms.

The remaining portion of this session is spent brainstorming various social skills participants believe students must learn if they are to work in cooperative groups. They classify the social skills as basic (skills that are a must for using a cooperative learning group) and advanced (social skills that can be taught once the basic skills are in evidence). Their list is then compared to the list we have generated from our work with many groups of teachers, which is found on page 38.

Session 7

Monitoring, intervening, processing, and evaluating are the focal points of this session. What monitoring means, how it is accomplished, and how to do it are the major points covered. To help with this topic, two groups role play a cooperative learning activity while all other members of the class monitor it. At the conclusion of each role play, a discussion is held on the skills involved in the activity.

When to intervene and how to intervene are covered before the major topic of processing. Participants spend a fair amount of time exploring this topic. Examples of individual, small group, and whole class processing are then presented to participants.

Perhaps the most difficult task of cooperative learning is to evaluate the outcomes of the lessons. The whole concept of evaluation is discussed, paying particular attention to procedures for evaluating group work. This session usually generates considerable discussion among participants.

Session 8

The topic of this session is teaching social skills. After discussing why and how these skills can be taught, participants are placed into small groups to "act out" several of them, based on what they might or might not sound or look like. In addition to the role playing, a number of the activities that can be used to teach social skills are presented.

Session 9

This session begins with participants doing the Thingamajig activity. (See pp. 53–55.) They are then shown the remainder of the Body Systems lesson plan on the overhead. At this point, they are asked to complete their lesson/project begun earlier. Finally, participants are asked to write down any questions/concerns they may have for which they would like a response.

Session 10

The final session begins with responses to the written questions from the previous session. These usually generate considerable discussion, which is a good opportunity for the instructors to stress the main points of the concept of cooperative learning. The session concludes with participants sharing their completed lesson/project plan.

Alternatives to Sessions 9 and 10

Cooperative learning is best taught during the school year when participants can try out a lesson with the assistance of the instructors. If time is available between Session 8 and the remaining two sessions, we suggest that participants be required to design a lesson, teach it, evaluate it, and report to the class. To ensure a successful beginning, we ask each participant to present his/her lesson plan to us before teaching it. Then sessions 9 and 10 are redesigned to allow the reports and discussions to take place.

APPENDIXES

A. COOPERATIVE LESSON/PROJECT PLANNING FORM

Grade Level: _____
Subject Area: _____

Lesson/Project Title: _____

A. General Objectives
   1. _____
   2. _____

B. Making Decisions
   1. Group size: _____

   2. Procedure for assignment to groups: _____
   _____

   3. Classroom arrangements needed: _____
   _____

   4. Resources needed: _____
   _____

   5. Types of group cohesion
      a. _____
      b. _____
      c. _____
      d. _____

C. Preparing the Lesson/Project

  1. Academic

    a. Specific objectives (will become daily objectives)

      (1) _____

      (2) _____

      (3) _____

      (4) _____

    b. Prerequisite knowledge and skills (to be taught or reviewed)

      (1) _____

      (2) _____

      (3) _____

  2. Social

    a. Creating group cohesion (these are the procedures for developing the items in B.5)

      (1) _____

      (2) _____

      (3) _____

      _____

   b. Role assignment and responsibilities

      (1) _____

      (2) _____

      (3) _____

3. Procedures for creating individual accountability

   a. _____

   b. _____

   c. _____

4. Specific social skills to be reviewed

   a. _____

   b. _____

   c. _____

5. Social skills that need to be taught (include behaviors that demonstrate these skills)

   a. _____

   b. _____

   c. _____

D. Monitoring Procedures and Observation Forms Needed

   1. _____

    2. _____

    3. _____

E. Processing Procedures to be Used

    1. _____

    2. _____

    3. _____

F. Evaluation

    1. Individual performance _____

    _____

    2. Group performance _____

    _____

    3. Social skills performance_____

    _____

    4. Procedure for determining composite grade for the lesson/project _____

    _____

B. ADDITIONAL SAMPLE LESSON PLANS

The following cooperative learning lesson plans were designed by members of classes we have taught. Each was asked to use the format given in Appendix A that we designed and to critique the lesson upon teaching it.

We realize the brevity of the plans, which may make it difficult for the reader. However, the general framework of each of the lessons should be grasped.

Subject Area: Language Arts
Grade Level: 6
Lesson/Project Title: Creative Writing
Teacher: Ruth Gilbertson
School: Menomonie School District

A. General Objective: To write original stories for our Elementary Creative Arts Magazine
B. Making Decisions
   1. Group size: Three or four
   2. Procedure for assignment to groups: High-, middle-, low-ability; did not mix sexes
   3. Classroom arrangements needed: Designate room areas; students move desks together
   4. Resources needed: Paper, pencil
   5. Types of group cohesion: Goal, role, environment
C. Preparing the Lesson/Project
   1. Academic
      a. Specific objectives
         (1) Determine at least one story theme for each pupil in the group
         (2) Students will be able to edit their writings efficiently
      b. Prerequisite knowledge and skills
         (1) Understand science fiction and modern realistic fiction
         (2) Be familiar with the elements of a short story
   2. Social
      a. Creating group cohesion
         (1) Goal: All write original stories; share stories orally in groups
         (2) Environment: Groups assigned to various parts of the room
      b. Role assignment and responsibilities
         (1) Leader: Keeps group on task and all involved; works on eye contact

(2) Secretary: Writes down ideas/themes as group brainstorms, edits
(3) Coach: Provides positive statements regarding ideas of group members; uses first names when encouraging

3. Procedures for creating individual accountability
Input of individual recorded by secretary. Teacher checks to be sure everyone has contributed at least one idea. Each student completes a piece of writing.
4. Specific social skills to be reviewed
   a. No put-downs
   b. Using quiet voices
   c. Staying with the group
5. Social skills that need to be taught
   a. Listening: Demonstrate what is meant by listening skills by using Activity 2, Drawing, page 46
   b. Encouraging: Class discussion on what is meant by encouraging
   c. Everyone contributing

D. Monitoring Procedures
   1. Monitoring procedures and observation forms needed
   Teacher moves from group to group observing the input from members of the group

E. Processing: Questions regarding social skills will be discussed daily with the class

F. Evaluation
   1. Individual performance: Completion of a piece of writing
   2. Group performance: Degree of positive interaction
   3. Social skills performance: Observation sheet on two skills—encouraging, listening
   4. Procedure for determining composite grade for the lesson/project: Completion of a piece of writing on the due date awards an A grade, including the practice of social

skills and contributions to the group effort, for the individual student provided he/she performed and contributed to the group.

Comments on the Lesson

After assignment of students to the various groups, we talked about how important it was to move into groups quietly. Using no put-downs had been addressed on a number of occasions by the guidance counselors. It has now become a part of the classroom vocabulary so it was only necessary to give a reminder. Our first session was to generate story themes for science fiction or realistic modern fiction. It was interesting to note the different approaches the various groups took. Much talking (quiet) went on in one group and it was apparent that members were hard at work. This particular group ended with a brief summary of what each member intended to write. Members' satisfaction with what they had accomplished was apparent. In contrast, another group jotted down titles rather than themes or short summaries. Members felt comfortable with this. Another group found itself floundering for themes. In the end I intervened and helped this group do some brainstorming by asking specific questions.

The cooperative lessons did not occur on consecutive days because most actual writing was done individually. I allowed two days for independent writing. These sessions were approximately 30 minutes. During this time I needed to conference with those students who were having trouble getting going. I listened to their ideas and provided alternatives. Some needed continual support as they went through the process.

Subject Area: Art
Grade Level: 6
Lesson/Project Title: Paper Letter Landscape
Teacher: Heidi Isusee
School: Hayward Middle School

A. General Objective: Students will create a "realistic" or "abstract" construction paper landscape using 16 letters of the alphabet
B. Making Decisions
   1. Group size: Four
   2. Procedures for assignment to groups: Mixed abilities—high, middle, low—and student survey indicating persons with whom students would like to work
   3. Classroom arrangements needed: Move tables to separate groups
   4. Resources needed: 24" by 36" piece of construction paper (colored), glue, scissors, scrap paper from scrap box, 16 templates for alphabet letters from each group member
   5. Types of group cohesion: Goal, resource task, role
C. Preparing the Lesson/Project
   1. Academic
      a. Specific objectives
         (1) Students will learn and practice roles of leader, checker, praiser, and expediter while doing Thingamajig sculpture and playing Art Rummy on consecutive days
         (2) Students will learn to cut paper letters (4 1/2" x 3")
         (3) Students will create a realistic or abstract landscape using 24" x 36" paper, scissors, glue, scrap paper, and 4 1/2" x 3" cut paper letters
      b. Prerequisite knowledge and skills
         (1) Knowledge of terms: landscape, abstract, realistic (reviewed and discussed)
         (2) Use of scissors and cutting procedures

2. Social
    a. Creating group cohesion
        (1) Goal: To create a landscape
        (2) Roles were learned (practiced) in Thingamajig sculpture
        (3) Resource: Each member brings 16 previously cut letters
    b. Role assignment and responsibilities
        (1) Leader: Keeps group on task; makes sure group is finished in 30–35 minutes, explains project at end
        (2) Checker: Checks for agreement before expediter can build; makes sure everyone signs back of project
        (3) Expediter: Obtains materials and glues parts to 24" by 36" paper according to group instructions.
        (4) Praiser: Encourages other students and turns in project to teacher after checker finishes
3. Procedures for creating individual accountability: Evaluation of the landscape developed from 16 alphabet letters
4. Specific social skills to be reviewed
    a. Use quiet voices (12-inch voices)
    b. Stay at your table
5. Social skills that need to be taught
    a. Everybody helps. Practice through use of monitors, in evaluating clean up, and use of specific jobs in previous projects
    b. No put-downs. Emphasized in guidance classes. Brainstorm statements of respect and praise
D. Monitoring Procedures
    1. Monitoring procedures and observation forms needed
        a. Check sheet with groups and roles listed
        b. Keep tally of comments made or heard that relate to social skill requirements while group builds the landscape
E. Processing
    1. Processing procedures to be used

      a. Class discusses hardships and difficulties encountered
      b. Individual evaluation of group and individual social skills used
      c. Group paragraphs about project
      d. Teacher comments on how students worked together treating each other with respect
F. Evaluation
   1. Individual performance
      a. Sixteen cut paper letters
      b. Individual evaluation sheet
   2. Group performance: Group landscape and written paragraph
   3. Social skills performance: Check sheet on skills
   4. Procedure for determining composite grade for the lesson/project: Project grade = group landscape + individual evaluation points + cut paper letter points + group-written paragraph

Comments on the Lesson

    Before I formed groups, I surveyed students using the following format:

- Name one or two students in the classroom whom you feel you can work with.
- Name one or two students in the classroom whom you feel you cannot work with.
- List the number of students in a group that you feel is best for your learning (size of group).

    This lesson was presented to classes of sixth graders and one class of seventh graders. The sixth graders felt the two hardest roles to play were the praiser and the expediter. Many felt it was hard not to use a put-down in praising and hard not to touch the objects in the sculpture. I saw some interesting and original sculptures created. Labeling the sculpture with a title gave many groups a goal to build toward.

I felt that the projects were very creative and successful; they are hanging on the bulletin board in the front of our classroom.

Most students did not know what I meant by "cooperative learning in small groups" and needed an introduction. I found the playing of the roles before the final project was a great help. I did see evidence of students making an effort to play the roles with each other while doing the project.

Students who were present for the letter cutting, but not the cooperative group work, had their letters used by the group. Students who were absent during the letter cutting, cut and contributed half the number of letters (eight) on the second day while working on the group project.

Most students said they felt the project was successful overall—including the social roles. Some students thought it was great that the overly active students were given the roles of expediters. Some students thought the idea of a "12-inch" voice was great! A few students wondered why I was teaching "Quest" ideas in art class. Most wanted to know when we would do it again, only change people in groups!!

Subject Area: English
Grade Level: 7
Lesson/Project Title: Newspaper
Teacher: Sharon Nelson
School: Chetek Middle School

A. General Objectives
   1. Students will construct a newspaper
   2. Students will identify parts of a newspaper
B. Making Decisions
   1. Group size: Three

2. Procedure for assignment to groups: Teacher assigned—high-, average-, low-ability in each group
3. Classroom arrangements needed: Move desks to groups of three
4. Resources needed: Markers, rulers, newsprint/paper, scissors, dictionaries, stencils, pens, letters, glue, erasers, whiteout, newspapers for format, student evaluation form, checklist
5. Types of group cohesion: Goal, identity, task, and role

C. Preparing the Lesson/Project
   1. Academic
      a. Specific objectives: Students will write articles with the following characteristics:
         (1) No misspellings
         (2) Correct punctuation
         (3) Proper capitalization
         (4) Similar ideas grouped in same paragraph
         (5) Five W's included and identified in copy
      b. Prerequisite knowledge and skills
         (1) Ability to write complete sentences and punctuate them
         (2) Ability to organize ideas into paragraphs
         (3) Understanding of the five W's
   2. Social
      a. Creating group cohesion
         (1) Goal: Group must work together to create a newspaper
         (2) Identity: Each group names its paper
         (3) Task: Students choose part of paper they can complete
         (4) Roles: Recorder, checker, coach
      b. Role assignment and responsibilities
         (1) Recorder: Writes down information group decides on

        (2) Checker; Checks spelling, punctuation, and grammar
        (3) Coach: Keeps group on task making sure each person contributes to the final product; also watches the clock
    3. Procedures for creating individual accountability
       a. Peer pressure
       b. Teacher observation tally
       c. Final construction of paper
    4. Specific social skills to be reviewed
       a. Talk in quiet voices
       b. Keep parts to self
       c. Stay with your group, respect opinion of others
    5. Social skills that need to be taught
       a. Solve problems without arguing—teach steps in conflict resolution
       b. Treat each other with respect—brainstorm examples of described behavior and verbal exchanges
       c. No put-downs
D. Monitoring Procedures
    1. Monitoring procedures and observation forms needed
       a. Check tally—keep tally of conflict resolution
       b. Respect each other's ideas in words, actions, and body language
       c. Each day I told students the specific social skills I was listening for as I circulated around the room. I made positive notes next to each of the groups, and shared these the following day
E. Processing
    1. Student evaluation sheet—similar to Body Systems evaluation form
    2. Class discussion about previous day's tally and notes
    3. Discussion with groups of their difficulties
    4. Final checklist

F. Evaluation
  1. Individual performance
     a. Student assessment of others in the group
     b. Teacher observation
  2. Group performance: Finished newspaper grade is received by each group member
  3. Social skills performance
     a. Observation by teacher
     b. Final product is a result of using social skills
  4. Procedure for determining composite grade for the lesson/project
     a. Students will receive the letter grade of their group's paper except people who typed the paper may receive the next higher letter grade or a plus (+), and students who didn't do their part in the group or who didn't follow the social rules of the class will have their grade dropped a letter or have a minus (–) added to it.

Comments on the Lesson

My first decision was that my groups were going to include three students whenever possible. I chose a high-, average-, and low-ability student to complete each group. I've had these students all year so I kept in mind their cliques and foes. In a couple of the sections where the numbers didn't come out right, I noticed the group didn't function as effectively with a fourth person.

The week before beginning the newspaper was spent discussing and practicing the social skills necessary for this project to fly.

The student evaluation form was a real eye-opener. Ninety-nine percent of the students said they liked the project. Many said it really wasn't work, but it was. I was surprised by the number of students who said they worked with somebody they didn't really know. I just assumed they all knew each other. They also said it was fun to work together. Students are very perceptive. A sampling of comments include: "He has lots of good ideas, but he needs to know when to stop goofing around." "She needs to learn to express herself, etc." This has been an interesting project to combat the winter blahs, and I continue to look for new ways to use cooperative learning groups.

Subject Area: Math
Grade Level: 7
Lesson/Project Title: Problem-Solving Activities
Teacher: Diane Johnson
School: Thorp Middle School

A. General Objectives
   1. To use, identify, and evaluate different problem-solving strategies
   2. To develop, observe, and cooperatively discuss solving problems with other members of the group
B. Making Decisions
   1. Group size: Three
   2. Procedure for assignment to groups: Students grouped at random but I will keep in mind their problem-solving abilities, selecting groups with at least one member with good reasoning skills
   3. Classroom arrangements needed: I have large tables in my room that smaller groups can easily use. Computers must be brought in from other classrooms for Day three
   4. Resources needed: Computers, Minnesota Educational Computing Consortium (MECC) disks, worksheets (all included), overhead transparency, felt squares, squares for smaller felt squares to fit on
   5. Types of group cohesion: Role, task, reward, and goal
C. Preparing the Lesson/Project
   1. Academic

a. Specific objectives
      (1) Identify and demonstrate different problem-solving strategies
      (2) State advantages and disadvantages of strategies used
      (3) Complete worksheets to solve problems
      (4) Identify number sequences
      (5) Estimate in multiplication
   b. Prerequisite knowledge and skills
      (1) Knowledge of some computer skills
      (2) Understand how to use charts or tables to organize data
2. Social
   a. Creating group cohesion
      (1) Positive role cohesion will be promoted by specific roles the group will need
      (2) All students must sign worksheets when they have finished to indicate all agree with answers
      (3) Group with best score for map-making activity receives some candy
      (4) Calling randomly on one member to explain the group's answer
   b. Role assignment and responsibilities
      (1) Checker: Checks to see that everyone always agrees with answer. Also reviews material for completeness when turned in
      (2) Material handler: Gets any resources that group needs to complete lesson including computers; is also responsible for returning material
      (3) Encourager: Provides encouragement for all group members. Also provides help to get *all* members to participate
3. Procedures for creating individual accountability
   a. Students will have a quiz on different strategy skills at the end of the lessons
   b. Students will put initials on all worksheets turned in to

        indicate their agreement with answers
- 4. Specific social skills to be reviewed
  - a. Stay in area
  - b. Work quietly
  - c. Follow classroom rules
  - d. Get in and out of groups in an orderly manner
- 5. Social skills that need to be taught
  - a. Accept constructive criticism
  - b. No put-downs
  - c. Include everyone in group
  - d. Encourage group members
  - e. Use materials appropriately

D. Monitoring Procedures

I will observe by walking around the classroom and keep tally marks of positive social behaviors observed

F. Evaluation
  1. Individual performance: Students will take a quiz
  2. Group performance
     a. Group will be graded on two different aspects—a grade on answers received on worksheet and a grade on performance of roles
  3. Social skills performance
  4. Procedure for determining composite grade for the lesson/project
     a. Three grades will be given for the lessons
        (1) On the quiz identifying different aspects of the strategies.
        (2) On the assignment itself, for worksheets completed
        (3) More subjective, on my observation of the student's behavior within the group (observation sheets will be used to determine this)

Comments on the Lesson

I had a fabulous time using cooperative learning in my classroom. I have my students in cooperative learning groups constantly. I use them not only during story problems but also during review before tests. I modify what was presented to us in a way that works wonderfully for me. In reviewing, students compete against the other groups in the class. I give review problems for each group to answer and I call upon anyone in the group not only to give the answer but also to tell how the group got the answer. This forces all students to work together and make sure that everyone in their group knows how to get the answer. It makes what used to be a hard assignment fun and easy to do. It gives me such great satisfaction to see students helping other students understand how to get an answer. As for the cooperative lessons that I wrote, I will give an evaluation of what worked well for me and what didn't.

I found with many of the lessons I didn't have enough time. We have ability grouping at our school and I found that the upper-ability group could get through what I wanted but the lower-ability class could not. Sometimes we barely got into the lesson. I still haven't figured out how to solve this except for adjusting the lessons in minilessons of some type. I have found now after doing quite a few cooperative learning activities that I don't need to take as much time to explain all the roles, but just review, and that helps.

As for the groups working cooperatively together, they did an excellent job. I feel, though, that it had a lot to do with the fact that I have always used grouping in my classes. I found out now that if I just happen to group students without assigning roles they will ask what the roles are going to be. I found a variety of personal ties in each class and some classes work much better than others. I would strongly urge anyone who has tried cooperative learning with only one group of students to make sure to try it again. I have the advantage of trying it with a variety of classes. I'm still having difficulty with one of the six classes, but am determined to get the students to work cooperatively with one another; I will keep plugging away.

I always am amused by developing the lesson plans step by step and finding out that I hardly follow them because the class figures out step nine while I am still on step two; I find myself constantly being flexible and going with the flow, just making sure all aspects are touched on. The lesson format itself is great.

As for the overall evaluation, I love cooperative learning in my classroom and I know that the students also love it. I feel that the students learn much more in their groups than on their own. I think that cooperative learning should be a part of every teacher's strategy.

Subject Area: Social Studies
Grade Level: 5
Lesson/Project Title: President Project
Teacher: Teresa Robinson
School: Rice Lake Area Schools

A. General Objectives
   1. To learn about a U.S. president
   2. To use research and report writing skills
B. Making Decisions
   1. Group size: Two
   2. Procedure for assignment to groups: Teacher-assigned, mixed ability
   3. Classroom arrangements needed: Move desks together
   4. Resources needed: Books on U.S. presidents, encyclopedias, construction paper, scissors, glue, magazines, markers, pencils, pens, papers
   5. Types of group cohesion: Goal, role, task, identity

C. Preparing the Lesson/Project
  1. Academic
     a. Specific objectives
        (1) Research president using resource materials and write answers to questions
        (2) Write a report by compiling answers to research question
        (3) Make a poster using words and pictures to represent president
        (4) Study and know last names of U.S. presidents
     b. Prerequisite knowledge and skills
        (1) How to use resource materials
        (2) How to write a research report
        (3) Knowledge of terms: political party, first lady
  2. Social
     a. Creating group cohesion
        (1) Goal: Group will work together to complete report, poster, and worksheets on specific areas
        (2) Task: Each member responsible for portion of research, poster, worksheets
        (3) Identity: Group has sense of identity related to president being researched
     b. Role assignment and responsibilities
        (1) Leader: Watches the time; keeps group on task and in its area
        (2) Checker: At end of each class period, checks to see assignments are in folder; checks over report before it is handed in
  3. Procedures for creating individual accountability
     a. Each member must research 5 of the 10 questions and write half of report
     b. Each member must complete 5 of the 10 questions
     c. Each person must list three facts about each president being reported on
     d. Each person receives grade on quiz on presidents' names

4. Specific social skills to be reviewed
   a. Using quiet voices
   b. Staying in your own area
   c. Staying on task
5. Social skills that need to be taught
   a. Respond to the signal: Practice turning off the light and having groups stop talking and look at teacher
   b. Treat others with respect: Brainstorm what treating others with respect looks and sounds like, and what it doesn't look and sound like

D. Monitoring Procedures
   1. Monitor quiet voices and staying in area and on task as a review—tally these behaviors at timed intervals
   2. Monitor roles and responding to signal—observe and cite examples of good role playing and responding to signal
   3. Monitor treating others with respect—cite specific examples of students using this behavior and ask students to cite examples

E. Processing
   1. Tally positive behaviors at timed intervals and relay this number
   2. Write examples of good role playing and responding to signal and state these examples to students
   3. Write examples of students treating each other with respect
   4. Have students quote examples of respectful treatment

F. Evaluation
   1. Individual performance
      a. List three facts on each president being reported on
      b. Quiz on each president reported on
      c. Quiz on names of presidents
   2. Group performance
      a. Report using resource material to answer questions
      b. Poster using pictures and words to represent the president
      c. Presentation of report and poster

3. Social skills performance—part of group evaluation processing
4. Procedure for determining composite grade for the lesson/project (see evaluation form, p. 31)

Comments on the Lesson

In other years I had done something similar to this as a small group project. However, by carefully implementing the elements of cooperative learning, this project developed into a far more positive learning experience, academically and socially, than it had ever been before.

Now, when I consider the basic elements of a cooperative learning lesson, I realize that face-to-face interaction was the only one that I had used before in small group work. With individual accountability and group cohesion built into this project, academic productivity increased unquestionably. Previously, I had simply given the assignment to the group and then had given students a group grade for the project. Then I had to play watchdog to see that students were dividing up the work equally. Of course, the "wood ticks" found ways to avoid working. The other students wanted a good grade, so they took over the majority of the work. But considering individual accountability, I redesigned the project so that each group member was responsible for answering 5 of the 10 questions and writing half of the report. The group members became positively interdependent and worked toward a group goal. Rather than let the wood ticks do minimal work, students now encouraged their partners to do their share. They realized that each person had a responsibility and a contribution to the grade that the group would receive. Furthermore, the evaluation form, which I had never used before, detailed the breakdown of the group grade so that students were aware of where their grade was coming from. I was pleased to see the increase in the amount of meaningful work being done.

Watching this progress, I felt confident that students were achieving the academic objectives. This structure and organization caused the project to run more smoothly than ever before, and gave me time to concentrate on introducing and monitoring social skills, which was a new focus for both the students and myself.

Overall I was thrilled with the results of the cooperative learning lesson. I found that considering the basic elements of cooperative learning, I could plan my lesson to run more smoothly, and to produce more academically and socially. Problem solvers were built into the planning of the lesson. At the same time students enjoyed what they were doing.

Subject Area: Science
Grade Level: 6
Lesson/Project Title: Building Circuits and Testing Conductors
Teacher: Cindy Huftel
School: Weyerhaeuser School District

A. General Objectives
   1. To understand the difference between a closed and open circuit
   2. To understand the function of a switch
   3. To understand what makes a good conductor
B. Making Decisions
   1. Group size: Four
   2. Procedure for assignment to groups: Teacher-assigned (two high ability, two low ability)
   3. Classroom arrangements needed: Groups of four desks
   4. Resources needed: Four of each of the following: D-cell batteries, battery holders (D-cell), bag full of insulated copper wire pieces with insulation removed from each end, light sockets, light bulbs, doorbells, switches, pieces of

cardboard, thumbtacks (8 total), pieces of bare copper wire, pieces of paper, combs, keys, wooden pencil, metal paper clips, rubber bands, and small screwdrivers
5. Types of group cohesion: Roles, goal, task, outside enemy/reward

C. Preparing the Lesson/Project
 1. Academic
    a. Specific objectives
       (1) The students will make predictions
       (2) The students will construct open and closed circuits
       (3) The students will draw a closed circuit
       (4) The students will open and close a circuit using a switch
       (5) The students will be able to deliver a good conductor/poor conductor
       (6) The students will be able to give examples of poor and good conductors
    b. Prerequisite knowledge and skills
       (1) Introduce the term *circuit*
 2. Social
    a. Creating group cohesion
       (1) Goal: Build a circuit that works and a conductor tester
       (2) Task: Each person builds a different part of the circuit or can touch only certain items
       (3) Outside Enemy/Reward: The first group to complete the assignment goes to lunch first
    b. Role assignment and responsibilities
       (1) Leader: Keeps the group on task and an eye on the clock
       (2) Materials Handler: Picks up all materials needed and returns them at end of class
       (3) Recorder: Records predictions on worksheets before doing experiments and filling out circuit worksheet
       (4) Checker: Makes sure that everyone in group agrees

to all predictions and final answers
- 3. Procedures for creating individual accountability
    - a. 1st day: Quiz—drawing a closed circuit
    - b. 2d day: Quiz—exploring how an electrical switch works
    - c. 3d day: Quiz—defining "good conductor, "poor conductor," and listing two examples of each
- 4. Specific social skills to be reviewed
    - a. Listening
    - b. Using quiet voices
- 5. Social skills that need to be taught
    - a. 1st day: Staying on task (practice mental math before science time)
    - b. Staying with group (basically will discuss with class why students think this is important if the job is to get done)

D. Monitoring Procedures
  1. Monitoring procedures and observation forms needed
     Check list with each group listed. I'll keep tallies of every time I observe the group keeping on task and students staying with the group. I also want to keep a tally on how the checker does, as this is a new role.

E. Processing
   Students will discuss what social skills they need more work on and if they had any problems in their group
   1. Processing procedures to be used
      - a. 1st day: Class discusses how students did with quiet voices
      - b. 2d day: Each group grades itself on how well members did on listening
      - c. 3d day: Individuals grade themselves and each other on staying on task and staying with the group

F. Evaluation
   1. Individual performance: Scores on the individual quizzes given each day
   2. Group performance: Single worksheet from each group
   3. Social skills performance: Check sheet on skills and I'll look

at how the groups and individuals evaluated themselves
4. Procedure for determining composite grade for the lesson/project: Students' scores on their quizzes and on their worksheets will be recorded in the grade book

Comments on the Lesson

A nice thing about cooperative learning—students really teach each other, but when they do need you, you're there and not back at your desk.

The students enjoyed their three days, and I especially loved having to grade only four worksheets each day instead of sixteen. Would I use cooperative learning again in my classroom? Yes, in fact I'm already trying to figure out where I can use it. Why? Because the children enjoyed it, and we both learned a lot.

Thank you for giving me another tool to help students learn and to help me become a better teacher. Cooperative learning is work, but well worth the effort.

Subject Area: Library
Grade Level: 5
Lesson/Project Title: Using *The Reader's Guide*
Teacher: Betty Bechman
School: Hayward Middle School

A. General Objectives
   1. To acquaint students with *The Reader's Guide to Periodical Literature* as a useful reference tool
   2. To show the value of using periodicals to give the most recent information
B. Making Decisions
   1. Group Size: Two
   2. Procedure for assignment to groups: Teacher-assigned
   3. Classroom arrangements needed: Move desks into groups

      4. Resources needed: *Reader's Guide*, ditto sheets
      5. Types of group cohesion: Goal, role, task
  C. Preparing the Lesson/Project
      1. Academic
         a. Specific objectives
            (1) Students will be able to use Guidelines for Using *The Reader's Guide*
            (2) Students will be able to identify the various parts of three entries from *The Reader's Guide*
      2. Social
         a. Creating group cohesion
            (1) Goal: Complete dittos
            (2) Role: Assign specific responsibilities
            (3) Task: Each student must be sure everyone in the group understands the parts of the entry
         b. Role assignment and responsibilities
            (1) Leader: Keeps group on task, agrees on answers
            (2) Recorder: Ensures that information is written on ditto
      3. Procedures for creating individual accountability
         a. Test
      4. Specific social skills to be reviewed
         a. Stay in seats
         b. Use quiet voices
      5. Social skills that need to be taught
         a. Stay on task
         b. No put-downs—use poster, use See 'Em-Hear 'Em-Do 'Em activity as large group on blackboard
  D. Monitoring Procedures
      1. Monitoring procedures and observation forms needed
         a. Use form with headings of quiet talk and no put-downs
         b. Use plus and minus signs to record behavior
  E. Processing
      1. Processing procedures to be used
         a. Group discussion at end of group work—point out good

       things and things to work on
      b. End of activity—self-evaluation
F. Evaluation
  1. Individual performance: Test
  2. Group performance: Two ditto sheets
  3. Social skills performance: Observations using forms
  4. Procedure for determining composite grade for the lesson/project
     a. Written test: 40%
     b. Two worksheets: 20% each (40%)
     c. Social skills: 20%

Comments on the Lesson

In the evaluation of group work five students didn't care for it. These students usually get good grades and prefer to work on their own. The other 17 students enjoyed group work. The following are some of the comments I received:

    I learned better ...
    ... fun to work together ...
    I learned to work with a person ...

Several students pointed out social skills areas they need more work on.

I found that observations were hard to do, especially when I needed to give a group guidance. Each day did get easier! I also observed that students who were absent had trouble fitting in with the group.

One error I made was not teaching the students a signal for quiet and attention. I realized this during the first day and did use the "lights off," but this should have been introduced the first day. I feel cooperative learning is easier to do when you have a regular classroom. I'm anxious to see how well it will work during my regular library schedule. Hopefully, it will be successful as I would like to set up more library lessons using cooperative learning. Because I have students just once a week I know I will have to spend more time on review, especially in classrooms where the teacher does not use the cooperative learning method. Time will tell.

Subject Area: English
Grade Level: 9
Lesson/Project Title: Advertising Project
Teacher: Emily Quisling
School: Chippewa Falls Middle School

A. General Objectives
   1. To understand types of ads found in newspapers
   2. To develop a book of ads
B. Making Decisions
   1. Group size: Three and four
   2. Procedure for assignment to groups: high-, middle-, low-abilities/personalities
   3. Classroom arrangements needed: Move furniture
   4. Resources needed: Magazines, newspapers, glue, scissors, typing paper, list of ad types
   5. Types of group cohesion: Goal, role, task
C. Preparing the Lesson/Project
   1. Academic
      a. Specific objectives
         (1) Label each ad correctly and organize it according to list
         (2) Place each ad neatly into book
      b. Prerequisite knowledge and skills
         (1) Ability to differentiate ad type
         (2) Ability to organize
   2. Social
      a. Creating group cohesion
         (1) Goal: Create finished advertising book

  (2) Roles: Materials handler, leader, checker
  (3) Task: Division of labor
 b. Role assignment and responsibilities
  (1) Materials handler: Gets glue, magazines, scissors, paper; helps find ads and puts everything away at end of period
  (2) Leader: Keeps group on task, helps find ads, does cutting and pasting
  (3) Checker: Helps find ads, makes final decision on correctness of choice, labels sheets after ad is glued, cleans floor
3. Procedures for creating individual accountability
 a. Each group member will receive same number of points for ad correctness and neatness
 b. Individual accountability will be determined by monitoring cooperation and the advertising section on the final test
4. Specific social skills to be reviewed
 a. Using quiet voices
 b. Listening to others' opinions
 c. Remaining on task
5. Social skills that need to be taught: Will use the skills enumerated in C.4.

D. Monitoring Procedures

I will monitor each group as a whole. But each individual will be monitored daily and will need to get two pluses (+'s) a day in order to earn all 24 points. Each day I will jot things down that need reviewing.

E. Processing

Talk with the class—ask questions: "What went well/poorly?" "What was helpful?" Ask general questions as appropriate to the classroom and problems or comments brought up to me during class period. Individual critique sheets turned in to me on Day 4.

F. Evaluation
1. Individual performance: Social interaction. Information will be tested on final test of newspaper unit.
2. Group performance
   a. Finished ad book/correctness
   b. Neatness of ad book
3. Social skills performance: Observation—checking in grade book
4. Procedure for determining composite grade for the lesson/project
   a. Each correctly labeled ad = 3 points (45 possible)
   b. Neatness = 15 points
   c. Social interaction = 24 points
   d. Total possible = 84 points

Comments on the Lesson

Never having been afraid of using small groups, I wondered why I was now afraid to try cooperative learning. How different could the two strategies be? Actually, there is a difference—a very nice difference!

My ninth graders first snickered and some laughed aloud when I began explaining what we would be doing. I mentioned that each of them would have a job to do, and that brought sideways glances. But the glances and rolling eyes subsided as I explained each job's importance, requirements, and the number of points each person could earn. This was on Day 0!

Day 1 got off to a slow start. It took a little bit for me to get everyone going. I was organized with the lessons and materials, but the furniture placement hadn't seemed to be such a problem. We have tables, not desks (I travel, too, from room to room) and most of the tables are long, not easily set up for group work.

Surprisingly, Day 1 ended without any major problems. Students took some time to get started, and they grumbled some, too, but cooperation did set in.

By Day 2 things were looking up. The students knew exactly what to do, and I was able to monitor more and answer questions less! I was beginning to like this. I walked around the room, paying attention to each person in each group. If each person received two +'s for the day, he or she then earned 8 points for the day. Students could earn a possible 8 points per day for a total of 24 points in social interaction.

Day 3 was a breeze—actually fun. The advertising books were finished on time and turned in. There was a healthy amount of bragging among the students. Later I graded the books on neatness and correctness of labeled ads.

I will try cooperative learning again. If I feel really brave, I will try it with eighth graders! The ninth graders were wonderful!

Subject Area: Math
Grade Level: 6
Lesson/Project Title: Multiplying Decimals
Teacher: Connie Cranford
School: South Middle School, Eau Claire

A. General Objectives: Students will learn, practice, and show mastery of multiplying decimals
B. Making Decisions
   1. Group size: Three
   2. Procedure for assignment to groups: Teacher-assigned mixed ability
   3. Classroom arrangements needed: Push desks together
   4. Resources needed: Math books, pencils, papers
   5. Types of group cohesion: Goal, reward, task
C. Preparing the Lesson/Project
   1. Academic
      a. Specific objectives
         (1) Days 1 and 2: Students will learn and practice multiplying decimals

        (2) Day 3: Students will show mastery of multiplying decimals
     b. Prerequisite knowledge and skills
        (1) Multiplication of three-digit numbers
        (2) Understanding value of decimals
  2. Social
     a. Creating group cohesion
        (1) Goal: To work together to complete assignments accurately
        (2) Reward: 50 points to each group member if all members complete all assignments for week
        (3) Role: Leader/checker
     b. Role assignment and responsibilities
        (1) Leader: Keeps group together, working at same pace
        (2) Checker: Reads answers out loud, compares numbers when answers vary
  3. Procedure for creating individual accountability
     a. Teacher monitors students with checklist
  4. Specific social skills to be reviewed
     a. Talk quietly
     b. Stay with group
  5. Social skills that need to be taught
     a. Helping one another with work
     b. Staying on task: (do sounds like/looks like)
D. Monitoring Procedures
  1. Checklist—points gained for talking quietly
  2. Points earned if all group members complete assignments
E. Processing
  1. Group discussion
  2. Self-evaluation
F. Evaluation
  1. Individual performance
     a. Some daily grades
     b. Quiz
  2. Group performance: One daily assignment taken randomly

characters.
4. Specific social skills to be reviewed
   a. Voice control
   b. On task, everyone participates
   c. No put-downs
   d. Sharing ideas
5. Social skills that need to be taught
   a. The four skills listed in C.4. will be introduced the day before this group activity

D. Monitoring Procedures
   1. Tallying for sharing ideas, everyone participating, and on-task behaviors
   2. Reinforcing good social skills

E. Processing
   1. Day 1: Written group evaluations, class discussion
   2. Day 2: Class discussion
   3. Day 3: Written individual evaluations and class discussion

F. Evaluation
   1. Individual performance: Quiz on characters
   2. Group performance: Group grade score on the number of characteristics found on all characters combined
   3. Social skills performance: Teacher deducts or adds points for group members on/off task, using or not using voice control, deducts for put-downs, and adds for helping other group members
   4. Procedure for determining composite grade for lesson/project
      a. 80%—character sheets for group
      b. 100%—quiz on characters
      c. 20%—social skills
      d. The grades on character sheets and social skills determine half the total grade; the quiz on characters the other half

Comments on the Lesson

Personally, I would like to comment on the tremendous amount of time I spent figuring out the groups for five different classes. I dwelt on it for four days, making continuous changes. In retrospect, I know it was the key to the week's success. I noticed only a couple of mistakes with grouping, and this did affect the total group performance, However, no discipline problems occurred.

My worst personal dilemma was absences. For students who were absent the first day of the lesson, I left holes in their groups for them to fill. I told all students present on the first day that they'd be responsible to have the information ready for their groups on Thursday, regardless of their excuses. They took me seriously, because mothers, brothers, and friends brought in assignments on that day for students who were out. Those who were absent the first two days received alternative assignments and I helped their groups fill in the missing information. This attendance problem was enough to make me not want to do a cooperative small group project again that lasted for more than one day.

I felt especially good about the social skills that we worked on. Each day I worried about how much noise we'd be making. (We are in an open building, and it is extremely easy to disturb other classrooms.) However, this year I have been blessed with the best behaved students I've had in 11 years, and they really tried to make the experience successful. All the discussion was on task and I very seldom had to take a point from a group for loud voices. I think the fact that students were looking for answers rather than discussing something controversial contributed to this result. I never heard a single verbal put-down from the 107 students who participated, but a few groups needed to work on sharing their ideas with each other.

In evaluating the final products, I found them to be more equal in quality than if they had been done individually. The lowest grade was a B-. I'm still uncomfortable giving all the students in a group the same grade. Having an individual quiz for students helped me feel better about it, but even that score was dependent on information given by other group members about their particular characters. Some students who would have gotten A's working by themselves got B's, and some usual C students got B's.

All in all, I felt the lessons were successful because we accomplished all our objectives both academically and socially, and still had fun. I'll definitely try another lesson soon.

Subject Area: Automotive Tech
Grade Level: 9 and 10
Lesson/Project Title: Safety and the Auto Shop
Teacher: Dave Fairbanks
School: Seymour High School

A. General Objectives
   1. Students will know safety rules and applications
   2. Students will be able to apply safety rules
B. Making Decisions
   1. Group size: Two
   2. Procedure for assignment to groups: Teacher-selected
   3. Classroom arrangements needed: Tables
   4. Resources needed: Safety rule sheet, problem card
   5. Types of group cohesion: Role, reward, outside enemy, goal
C. Preparing the Lesson/Project
   1. Academic
     a. Specific objectives
       (1) To be able to apply rules to shop machines
     b. Prerequisite knowledge and skills
       (1) Shop safety rules

    2. Social
        a. Creating group cohesion
           (1) Cooperation: All group members need to contribute for the group to win
           (2) Stay in group and on task
           (3) Shared feelings (of group against outside enemy)
           (4) Winner gets prize for most applications
        b. Role assignment and responsibilities
           (1) Leader, recorder, reporter
    3. Procedures for creating individual accountability
        a. Safety test at end for all students
    4. Specific social skills to be reviewed
        a. Use quiet voices
        b. Treat others with respect
    5. Social skills that need to be taught
        a. Cooperation
        b. Stay in group and on task
        c. Share feelings
D. Monitoring Procedure
    1. Teacher observation of individuals in groups
E. Evaluation
    1. Individual performance
    2. Group performance
        a. How many applications of the rules did we find?
        b. Do we know why safety rules exist?
    3. Social skills performance
        a. Not a part of final grade
    4. Procedure for determining composite grade for the lesson/project
        a. 75%—individual test grade
        b. 25%—composite of group average

Comments on the Lesson

    The lesson went so well, I am still in awe. There is little I would change if I did it again tomorrow. It was difficult for me, however, to walk around supervising without giving students answers when they got bogged down. I felt a little guilty standing there, encouraging them, but still keeping a distance. In some way, I felt I wasn't doing my teaching job. In the end, however, it came to me that my teaching was done in the preparation and summary of the lesson—not during the cooperation phase.

The final proof of my success was in the safety rule test the next day. Every student in the class, regardless of ability level, scored 90% or higher (which was my goal). I had planned to place 25% of their final grade on group average, but due to high scores, it wasn't necessary. The discussion about the lessons brought out many interesting points by some of the students. One said he thought the lesson was good because at the beginning of the year, it got him thinking about safety without being lectured to. Another felt it helped him to see different views and applications from students, not just the teacher. Almost all thought the time went fast, and the class was more interesting when they were actively involved.

My own feelings were similar, although I see cooperative learning as a method that should be used with my other methods of instruction. I was pleased to find that the method works well with secondary students, as it does in a middle-school situation. In fact, after discussion with my supervisor, I feel it could be used at any level with success.

I really was pleased with the student comprehension level in this specific lesson. Student safety in the shop and the liability factors involved raise my level of concern quite often. I feel more confident and secure because of the fact that I have prepared students as best I can to be safe, responsible individuals in a lab situation.

Subject Area: Science
Grade Level: 8
Lesson/Project Title: Topographic Map Reading
Teachers: Tom Day
　　　　　Bob Battista
School: Seymour Middle School

A. General Objectives
   1. Students will be able to relate pertinent information from their own topographic map
B. Making Decisions
   1. Group size: Three
   2. Procedure for assignment to groups: Teacher-assignment by ability (high, middle, low)
   3. Classroom arrangements needed: Regroup desks
   4. Resources needed: Center with various topographic maps, question sheets, and student textbook, paper and pencil
   5. Types of group cohesion: Goal, reward, role
C. Preparing the Lesson/Project
   1. Academic
      a. Specific objectives
         (1) Review and use various topographic map symbols
         (2) Review and use contour lines
         (3) Discover various special symbols used on topographic maps
         (4) Review and use latitude and longitude in locating a position
      b. Prerequisite knowledge and skills
         (1) Identify the type and use of topographic maps
         (2) Basic map symbols
         (3) Contour lines
         (4) Latitude and longitude
   2. Social
      a. Creating group cohesion
         (1) Goal: Complete one copy of a question sheet

       (2) Role: Leader, reader, recorder
       (3) Reward: Three best teams will receive extra credit test points (five)
    b. Role assignment and responsibilities
       (1) Leader: Keeps group on task
       (2) Reader: Reads questions in sequence
       (3) Recorder: Writes agreed-upon answers clearly on one copy
  3. Procedures for creating individual accountability
    a. Critique other's work by having to reach consensus
    b. Natural interest in mapped areas
    c. Individual motivation
  4. Specific social skills to be reviewed
    a. Stay on task
    b. Work quietly
    c. Stay in group
    d. Stay in roles
  5. Social skills that need to be taught
    a. Consulting group before teacher (discuss)
    b. Sharing and contributing ideas (role play/model)
D. Monitoring Procedures
  1. Checking to see everyone is actively involved and contributing
  2. Teacher observation (check sheet)
E. Processing: Ask students to respond to the following questions:
  1. What did you enjoy about working with maps of your area?
  2. What specific item did you find frustrating?
  3. How many have all your chips?
  4. Name some questions you would have gotten wrong if you were working by yourself.
  5. Name some question your group would have gotten wrong without your help.
  6. If you could change the cooperative learning structure, what would you change?

    7. What are the advantages of cooperative learning?
F. Evaluation
    1. Individual performance: Unit test
    2. Group performance: Group score—extra credit points to three best teams
    3. Social skills performance
        a. Check sheet/observation sheet
        b. "Chip method"
    4. Procedure for determining composite grade for the lesson/project
        a. Academic assignment score
        b. Effort score
        c. Test score and bonus points

Comments on the Lesson

    Overall, the class had a very positive reaction to the lesson. Work quality and productivity was at or above level for all students. Social skills development occurred as evidenced by the lack of reminders given and the lack of negative practice marks on the monitoring sheets. No effort "chips" were relinquished by any student during the three days. Cooperative learning proved to be an effective tool to use as one of many ways to present both social and academic instruction.

Subject Area: Language Arts/English
Grade Level: 5 or 6
Lesson/Project Title: Poetry
Teacher: Cherisma Larson
School: South Middle School

A. General Objectives
    1. Students will be able to identify one of four assigned poems
    2. Students will recognize three other forms of poetry as presented by other groups

B. Making Decisions
   1. Group size: Three and four
   2. Procedure for assignment to groups: Teacher-assigned, heterogeneous, mixed sex
   3. Classroom arrangements needed: Regroup desks
   4. Resources needed: Handout of one sample poem to each group, magic marker, large poster board or paper, tape or tacks for hanging
   5. Types of group cohesion: Goal, task, role
C. Preparing the Lesson/Project
   1. Academic
      a. Specific objectives
         (1) Compose collectively one type of poem and define it
         (2) Recognize three other forms of poetry through oral presentations
         (3) Evaluate group work
      b. Prerequisite knowledge and skills
         (1) Review various poetry structures
         (2) Each group is responsible for composing one type of poem: limerick, diamante, haiku, or quatrain
   2. Social
      a. Creating group cohesion
         (1) Goal: Each group member must understand structure and terminology of poem the group is working on
         (2) Role: Facilitator, reader/leader, secretary
         (3) Task: Each student is to create and be responsible for thinking of one or two lines to use to complete the poem
      b. Role assignment and responsibilities
         (1) Reader/leader: Keeps group on task, reads poem
         (2) Secretary: Writes agreed-upon lines of poem clearly on one copy
         (3) Facilitator: Handles materials

3. Procedures for creating individual accountability:
   a. Each student to be assigned to complete at least one (or more) line(s) for group poem
4. Specific social skills to be reviewed
   a. Everybody helps
   b. Use quiet voices
   c. Stay in group
5. Social skills that need to be taught
   a. Compromising: Define compromise, discuss daily situations that call for compromising. How is compromising done in your home? Discuss how some students in the group may not like suggestions offered by others as lines of poetry become complete, but by agreeing to use suggestions, compromising becomes a practice.

D. Monitoring Procedures
   1. Teacher circulates, providing feedback and reinforcement as needed; no formal form needed

E. Processing
   1. Teacher provides feedback from observations made and statements heard. Group processing of social skills used by students, rating group on a scale of 1–5 on the following social skills: everybody helps, quiet voices, stay with the group, listen, compromise

F. Evaluation
   1. Individual performance: None
   2. Group performance: Project completion
   3. Social skills performance: Teacher observation
   4. Procedure for determining composite grade for the lesson/project: No formal grading except complete/incomplete

Comments on the Lesson

This poetry lesson was well received by students because they could work cooperatively on a not-so-appealing lesson to this age group!

The charge was for each group to cooperatively compose one type of poem that had been assigned. Introducing compromising was a necessary social skill to implement in this lesson. Each group member was responsible for completing one or two lines of the poem assigned by the leader. Teammates could not approve another teammate's lines of the poem; this is where compromising skills were necessary.

After the poems were completed, they were posted in the room, and each group read and discussed its accomplishments. Believe it or not, students couldn't wait to share! Heartwarming for any teacher to watch a "blah" become an "aahh!"

C. POSTERS

In a classroom where cooperative learning is used, it is helpful to reinforce the ideas in many different ways. Creating posters or bulletin boards that emphasize the concepts is one way to help students internalize the ideas being taught. The following phrases are meant to spark ideas that teachers can transform into visual learning tools for the classroom. Or students can work in teams to create visuals that will reinforce the concepts being taught.

- Creating a cooperative climate:

    No one is as smart as all of us.

    Everybody helps.

    Share your ideas.

    When you hear the signal:
    1. Stop talking.

2. Look at the teacher.
  3. Be ready to listen.

Ask questions.

Help by telling how or showing how, NOT by giving answers.

The key to cooperation: WE instead of ME.

No put-downs.

- Processing:

  How could we do better next time?

  Do you talk as much as you listen?

  Do you listen as much as you talk?

  What did we learn today?

- Roles and responsibilities:

  The Secretary writes down the answers the group agrees upon.

  The Coach says: We'll get it! Nice try! Looks good! We can do it! Good work! Almost done! Super! We're going great! Wow!

  The Checker checks to make sure all group members understand and agree about:
  1. How to solve each problem
  2. The answers

  The observer records the actions of the group on an observation sheet.

SUGGESTED READING LIST

BOOKS

Adams, Dennis M., and Hamm, Mary E. *Cooperative Learning, Critical Thinking and Collaboration Across the Curriculum.* Springfield, Ill.: Charles C. Thomas, 1990.

Cohen, Elizabeth. *Designing Groupwork.* New York: Teachers College Press, 1986.

Dishon, D., and O'Leary, P. A. *Guidebook for Cooperative Learning.* Holmes Beach, Fla.: Learning Publications, 1984.

Fluegelman, Andrew, ed. *New Games Book.* New York: Doubleday, 1976.

Fluegelman, Andrew, ed. *More New Games.* New York: Doubleday, 1981.

Graves, Nancy, and Graves, Ted, eds. *Cooperative Learning: A Resource Guide.* Santa Cruz, Calif.: International Association for the Study of Cooperation in Education, 1987.

Johnson, D. W., and Johnson, R. *Learning Together and Alone: Cooperative, Competitive, and Individualistic Learning.* Englewood Cliffs, N.J.: Prentice Hall, 1987.

Johnson, D. W.; Johnson, R.; and Holubec, E. *Circles of Learning: Cooperation in the Classroom.* Rev. ed. Edina, Minn.: Interaction Book Co., 1986.

Johnson, D. W.; Johnson, R.; and Holubec, E. *Cooperation in the Classroom.* Edina, Minn.: Interaction Book Co., 1988.

Kagan, S. *Cooperative Learning: Resources for Teachers.* Riverside, Calif.: University of California, 1988.

Slavin, Robert. *Cooperative Learning.* New York: Longman, 1983.

Weinstein, Matt, and Goodman, Joel. *Playfair.* San Luis Obispo, Calif.: Impact Publishers, 1988.

ARTICLES

Augustine, Dianne K.; Gruber, Kristin D.; and Hanson, Lynda R. "Cooperation Works." *Educational Leadership,* December/January 1990.

Edwards, Claudia, and Stout, Judy. "Cooperative Learning: The First Year." *Educational Leadership,* December/January 1990.

Ellis, Susan S. "Introducing Cooperative Learning." *Educational Leadership,* December/January 1990.

Johnson, David W., and Johnson, Roger T. "Cooperative Small-Group Learning." *NASSP Curriculum Report,* October 1984.

Jones, M. Gail. "Cooperative Learning: Developmentally Appropriate for Middle Level Students." *Middle School Journal,* September 1990.

Logan, Thomas F. "Cooperative Learning: A View from the Inside." *Social Studies,* May/June 1986.

Nickolai-Mays, Susanne, and Goetsch, Kristine. "Cooperative Learning in the Middle School." *Middle School Journal,* November 1986.

Pearson, Craig. "Cooperative Learning: An Alternative to Cheating and Failure." *Learning,* March 1979.

Schniedewind, Nancy, and Salend, Spencer J. "Cooperative Learning Works." *Teaching Exceptional Children,* Winter 1987.

Slavin, Robert. "The Cooperative Revolution in Education." *Education Digest,* September 1988.

Smith, Roy A. "A Teacher's Views on Cooperative Learning." *Phi Delta Kappan,* May 1987.

Tyrrell, Ronald. "What Teachers Say About Cooperative Learning." *Middle School Journal,* January 1990.

Wynne, Edward A. "Teaching about Cooperation." *Phi Delta Kappan,* March 1983.